THE *FOCCUSSED* DECISION MAKER

A Quick and Easy Guide for Decision Making

TERRY BRESNICK AND OMAR PERIU

THE *FOCCUSSED* DECISION MAKER
A Quick and Easy Guide for Decision Making

Printed in the United States of America

Formatting and cover design by Debora Lewis arenapublishing.org.

ISBN-13: 978-1530516032
ISBN-10: 153051603X

If you want your next meeting or convention to be a guaranteed success and leave a lasting impression on your audience, email now for a free consultation and more information

Omar Periu

Omar Periu International, Inc.

Omar@OmarPeriu.com

www.OmarPeriu.com

Terry Bresnick

Bresnick@ix.netcom.com

www.innovativedecisionscapes.com

CONTENTS

Preface

Most people hate making difficult decisions. Most people are not very good at and need help in making such decisions. That is why we decided to write this book.

Terry Bresnick, a graduate of West Point, had many opportunities to apply the decision making processes he learned when serving as an Officer in the Army for 10 years of active duty and 18 more years in the U.S. Army Reserves. He has invested more than 40 years helping others make better decisions, primarily in large Government organizations and businesses, before going out on his own as an independent consultant and eventually retiring as CEO of his own firm. **Omar Periu** is a successful entrepreneur, an author, and an award-winning speaker who has spent more than a decade educating salespeople, leaders and entrepreneurs world-wide. He has delivered more than 5,000 seminars, workshops and training programs and has trained more than two million people in more than two-thirds of the Fortune 500 companies.

This book came about after Terry met Omar while attending one of Omar's seminars. Terry says, "As I looked around the room, and listened to the stories of the participants, it became obvious that many of the techniques that we were using to help large organizations could be just as relevant to these entrepreneurs." He spoke to Omar about it and the two entrepreneurs decided to collaborate on the *FOCCUSSED Decision Maker*. By making some easily implementable tools and thought processes available to those facing challenging decisions, we believe that we can make their lives better, easier and more productive. Many books on decision making are excellent, but they are very technical, very mathematical, and are intended for long, extended, and costly analyses. Our approach focuses on simplicity and usability, yet still emphasizes the key components of good decision making. We want this to be an enjoyable and easy read, yet with enough content to affect their ability and your ability to make better decisions.

In this book, you will learn how to become a **FOCCUSSED** decision maker. No, **FOCCUSSED** is not misspelled; it is an acronym for the following steps:

- Identify and properly **F**rame the decision or problem at hand

- Specify the goals, **O**bjectives, and values that you are trying to achieve

- Develop creative, meaningful **C**hoices from among which you can choose

- Evaluate the **C**onsequences of selecting each alternative using your goals, objectives, and values

- Think about the key **U**ncertainties that could impact the decision

- Understand the **S**waps and trade-offs that you are willing to make

- Develop an approach for implementing your **S**olution

- **E**licit the data you'll need from a variety of sources

- **D**isseminate and communicate your decisions to others.

As you read this book, you will see references to some great books that are available if you want to dig a bit deeper into the topics. We use endnotes indicated by bracket notation, [ ], to let you know where to find some of the material.

At the end of each chapter, we will present you with a rapid recap of the key concepts discussed in that chapter. These "quick and dirty" summaries should help you to remember what decision making is all about.

In many of the general explanations and examples in this book, we use the pronoun "we" which includes the combined experiences of both Terry and Omar. In certain cases that were unique experiences to just one or the other, we will refer to Terry or Omar by name.

Terry Bresnick

Omar Periu

Acknowledgments

Terry Bresnick:

There are many people who, without their tutelage, I could not have written this book. I would like to acknowledge Professors Ron Howard, Ed Sondik, and Jim Matheson, all of whom taught me the ABCs of Decision Analysis (DA) at Stanford University. Al Grum was my mentor as I started my career as a decision analyst in the Army and as an Assistant Professor at West Point. Rex Brown, Cameron Peterson, Roy Gulick and Larry Phillips helped me understand the importance of the "socio" side of decision analysis and molded my perspective on facilitation. Jim Chinnis brought me to Decision Sciences Consortium and gave me the freedom to develop my DA skills. Dennis Buede was first my boss when I left the Army, and later became my collaborator and partner for many years as we built Innovative Decisions, Inc. together. Greg Parnell has been a valued colleague and collaborator for many years, and I have learned much from him. I'd also like to thank Gary Parish and Wendi Runyon for reviewing the book and offering suggestions to help me improve it, and Aliza Bresnick for providing my cover photograph. I'm especially grateful to Omar Periu for spurring me on to write this book and for collaborating on it with me. But most of all, I'd like to acknowledge my wife Andrea, who has been by my side for the last 30 years and has helped me at every stage of writing this book. Her valued counsel and editing has made this a much better product, and she has truly been my partner in this effort.

Omar Periu:

There are many people who helped make this book a reality. Their knowledge, hard work, inspiration and dedication have made The *Foccussed* Decision Maker possible. First I would like to thank Terry Bresnick for his concepts, insights and inspiration to make this book come to life. Terry, it has been an honor and privilege to work with you on this project. Without you, this book would not have been written. A special thanks to Andrea Bresnick for her selfless support and guidance though-out this process. Your efforts helped tremendously. I would like to thank my mentor, Tom Murphy, for helping me to become the person I always wanted to be. A special thanks to my other mentors, Tom Hopkins and my mentors who are no longer with us but will always be a part of who I have become; Zig Ziglar and Jim Rohn. I would like to thank my wife Helen, who inspires me to continue the journey to live my dream of helping others, and to my Princess Alexandra and my little King Maxwell, who keep me young and motivate me on a daily basis with their love. I would like to give a special thanks to my parents, Nelida and Oduardo Periu, who always told me that I had greatness within me, even when I did not believe it myself–You are the reason I am who I am today. Most of all, I would like to express my appreciation to you, the reader for believing in the power of self-development. Using the materials in this book, you will become an amazing **FOCCUSSED** decision maker. Always remember, "Success is in the moment— make every moment count." And never be denied of the greatness you have within you.

About the Authors

Terry A. Bresnick is the President of Innovative Decision Analysis and is the co-founder and Senior Principal Analyst at Innovative Decisions, Inc. He has had more than 40 years of experience in applying decision analysis to complex problems of Government and Industry. Earlier, as an officer in the U.S. Army, and currently, as a consultant in the private sector, Terry has demonstrated his expertise in the areas of decision analysis, risk analysis, strategic planning, resource allocation and budgetary analysis, evaluation of competing alternatives, cost-benefit analysis, and business area analysis. He has facilitated more than 1000 decision conferences and/or workshops for Government and private sector clients. He has been an Assistant Professor of Systems and Decision Analysis at the U.S. Military Academy and is an Adjunct Instructor at the University of Arkansas. Terry is also a Certified Financial Planner, a Certified Analytics Professional, a Fellow of the Society of Decision Professionals, and a registered Professional Engineer. He received a B.S. in Engineering from the U.S. Military Academy, an M.B.A. in Decision Science from George Mason University, and an M.S. in Statistics and the Degree of Engineer in Engineering-Economic Systems from Stanford University. Terry is a retired Lieutenant Colonel from the U.S. Army.

Omar Periu proudly wears his rags to riches story for others to hear about and learn from. He went from $147 a month at age 21 as a personal trainer to multi-millionaire status by age 31. Omar and his family fled Castro's regime when he was only seven years old. They arrived in Miami with no money, no family or friends in America and nothing but what they were wearing when they arrived.

Enduring the taunting of other children, the cold winters of Illinois and the obstacle of language barriers, Omar didn't let it embitter him. Instead, he made the most of his situation. His father, reading from a tattered Spanish copy of Dale Carnegie's book, "How To Win Friends and Influence People," taught Omar an important life lesson. "It doesn't matter who you are, where you're from or what color you are, you can do anything you put your mind to."

Not knowing enough about success and its outcome, Omar sought out and studied the masters. He observed the difference between the performance of top achievers, successful entrepreneurs and those barely squeaking by making a living. From there, Omar developed his Zero to Wealth Systems™, The Investigative Selling Principles™, The One Minute Meeting Effective Presentation System™, and From Management to Leadership™ skills. Implementing these into his own career, he soon became one of the top professionals in his field.

By the time he turned 31, he owned some of the most profitable health clubs, sports medicine facilities and many other entrepreneurial successes in the United States. From his modest beginnings as a take-it-on-the-chin salesperson, Omar knew the pain of rejection and failure. He also discovered the high of mastering effective presentations, sophisticated closing skills, the power to influence and persuade, and most importantly, he is now teaching these unique success systems to entrepreneurs, salespeople and leaders all over the world. Like Omar's experience, having internalized these principles, his students are now reporting their greatest triumphs ever!

Omar's content is fresh and inspiring, his presentations impeccable, and his story unforgettable. He is now referred to as the number one "how-to" Motivational Teacher in the Americas, a world-traveled speaker who has spent over a decade educating entrepreneurs, salespeople, and leaders world-wide. Omar has personally delivered more than 5,000 seminars, workshops and training programs. He has trained more than two million people in more than two-thirds of the Fortune 500 companies.

Omar has been a featured speaker at events with superstars Zig Ziglar, General Colin Powell, Larry Bird, Harvey Mackay, Jim Rohn, Terry Bradshaw, Bob Proctor, Larry King, Robert Kiyosaki, Tony Robbins, Don Shula, Lou Holtz, Denis Waitley, and many, many more.

His articles are published in Success Magazine, Sales and Management Magazine, Selling Power Magazine, Martial Arts Success Magazine, and more. He has authored several books like The One Minute Meeting™, From Management to Leadership™, Get Real Get Rich™ and today's #1 book in sales, Investigative Selling™. He has been presented with the Business Man of the Year award for the State of Florida, by the Florida Business Advisory Council. He is on the Board of Directors to Wayne Huizenga's School of Entrepreneurs and Nova Southeastern University.

He is a member of the National Speakers Association and has been inducted into the prestigious International Platform Association. Most importantly, he has dedicated himself to helping others fulfill their dreams by teaching them how to achieve greatness!!!

Omar compassionately helps groups and individuals learn how to overcome fear, failure, and handle rejections. He will help you get out of the slump that holds you back from becoming a true champion with his inspiring stories and motivational precepts! Omar encourages you to face your fears, kick your counter-productive habits and become a calculated risk taker. He asks you to THINK about where you are now, where you WANT to be, and HOW to get there as quickly as possible.

Omar helps people build a better self, team and company with a fresh take on age-old solutions. He specifically teaches you how to set and achieve your desired goals while ensuring constant and never ending improvement.

Omar Periu is more than a motivator; his peers refer to him as "The Master Motivational Teacher." Omar brings audiences to their feet with his indefinable quality of magnetism.

To quote Omar's philosophy:

"Success is in the moment—so make every moment count!!!"

~Omar Periu

CHAPTER 1: INTRODUCTION

"If you obsess over whether you are making the right decision, you are basically assuming that the universe will reward you for one thing and punish you for another."

~Deepak Chopra, *The Book of Secrets: Unlocking the Hidden Dimensions of Your Life*

"I hate making decisions! It's so-o-o-o-o stressful!!"

That is what Terry hears from his youngest daughter whenever she has to make up her mind about something. And, unfortunately, her opinion is shared by many, whether it is an average person making a personal decision, a budding entrepreneur deciding on a new business venture, or even a high-level Government official deciding on programs that will affect millions of people.

After many, many years of helping people make decisions, Omar and Terry still often come across two very different attitudes about decision making. The first is best represented by a quote from the French Emperor Napoleon, who, in his *Maxims* of 1804 [1] wrote:

"Nothing is more difficult, and therefore more precious, than to be able to decide."

The counter balancing perspective comes from that great management guru, Dogbert, who, in his *Top Secret Management Handbook* [2] wrote:

"Nothing good ever came from a management decision.
Avoid making decisions whenever possible.
They can only get you in trouble."

Now for those of you who can relate and proscribe to the Dogbert perspective, you probably needn't read any further. We probably can't help you. But for the rest of you, keep reading - there is help on the horizon in terms of the **FOCCUSSED** decision making approach.

"A decision is a sharp knife that cuts clean and straight;
indecision, a dull one that hacks and tears
and leaves ragged edges behind it."

~Gordon Graham

Why do so many people fear making a decision? When a manager, an owner, or an investor faces a difficult decision, the obvious course is the clean and straight method mentioned in the above quotation. Yet people often let indecision rule, which leads inevitably to a torn and ragged outcome. We believe that there are four basic reasons that people fear making a decision:

One: The cost of a making a bad decision might be professionally, monetarily, and personally very high. Life savings may be involved in a business decision, and even lives themselves may hang in the balance in other decisions. Seven years ago, when Terry's oldest daughter was diagnosed with acute myeloid leukemia, she was faced with treatment decisions that had very nasty potential consequences, including death. *Spoiler alert* – great decisions were made by her and her doctors, the disease was eliminated thanks to a bone marrow transplant from a generous stranger, she is healthy, and she and her husband have just celebrated their sixth wedding anniversary! But, as you can imagine, thinking about the stakes and possible consequences each step of the way was extremely stressful. The doctors are the ones who can talk with expertise about the possible outcomes and their probabilities, but only the patient can know how he or she feels about the potential outcomes. In addition, we don't all feel the same, which means that decisions are personal and what is considered to be a good result for one person may be viewed as a bad result for another.

Two: More than one person may have a stake in the decision, and their respective goals and values may conflict with each other. One partner in a small business venture may want it to grow slowly and conservatively, while the other partner may want to go for the gold ring and aggressively take chances on opportunities that carry more risk but have potential for far greater rewards. For example, recently, Omar and one of his colleagues owned a business together. Omar wanted to move quickly, take on debt, and expand as quickly as possible. His partner believed in a business approach that was slow, steady, and conservative. We can't say that one owner is correct and that the other is wrong since they have conflicting objectives. But conflict is not necessarily a bad thing. In many cases, openly expressed conflict is a healthy business experience. We will address some of the most effective ways of handling conflict later in the book, but for now, just remember that each stakeholder deserves respect and a fair hearing – followed by a clearly stated and defensible decision.

Three: When we make a decision in the present, we are uncertain about how events will unfold in the future – we don't have the luxury of knowing what will happen with certainty. For example, if we are thinking of investing in a rental property to generate additional income, the results will depend on what percent of the time we can keep the property rented, the care tenants will take of the property, and the hidden surprises that often show up when we least expect them such as mold hidden behind the walls, the impact of hurricanes, the destruction from earthquakes, etc. If only we knew for sure what was going to happen, our job would be easy; unfortunately, we don't, and we have to figure out how to make good decisions knowing that the future is uncertain and much of it is outside of our control. Flipping a coin to deal with uncertainty just doesn't cut it, and we will need approaches to deal with what we all refer to as probability.

Four: We also must recognize and learn to work with people who have different attitudes towards decision making. Some are meticulous planners who never make a decision without employing a thought process that is logical, methodical, and quantitative. Others like to fly by the seat of their pants and follow their instincts when making a decision. Neither process is inherently right or wrong. Decision making is a very personal matter and is impacted by an incredible number of factors that affect the process. Those impacts may vary as widely as the number of people making the decisions. Working with people holding different attitudes is inevitable. It can be challenging and frustrating, but can also be rewarding. Later in the book, we'll show you some great tools and processes that can bring about those rewards!

WHAT IS A DECISION?

In order to talk about decisions and decision making, we first should define what we mean. One of Webster's definitions of a decision is the act of making up one's mind. That's about as basic as you can get. To keep it simple, for our purposes, a decision is the choice among alternatives, based on how we value and trade-off their pros and cons, made in the face of uncertainty about what will actually happen. We can think of the decision-making process as having three pillars supporting the decision maker:

- **preferences**–what we prefer, what meets our goals and objectives, and the recognition that preferences are personal to the one making the decision

- **alternatives** – the choices, options, or courses of action that we have, and over which we have some degree of control

- **information** – what we know about the situation, what we don't know, how we connect choices to outcomes, and how we deal with uncertainty.

DEFINING A GOOD DECISION

So how do you know if you have made a good decision? Let's first distinguish between what we mean by a good decision versus a good outcome. A *good outcome* is one that "feels good" – what we wanted to have happen, did happen, and we are very happy with the outcome that occurred. Contrast that with a *good decision* which is a choice that is consistent with the three pillars: the preferences that we are trying to achieve, the alternatives that we face, and the information that we know and don't know about the decision situation. Sometimes, we make choices that are totally inconsistent with the three pillars, but we get lucky and get the unexpected favorable result. This is the case where we make a **bad decision**, but get a **good outcome**. Sometimes, we make choices that are totally inconsistent with the three pillars, and we get terrible results (but, probably, no surprise). This is the case where we make a **bad decision** and get a **bad outcome**. Unfortunately, there are times when the decision that we make is totally consistent with the preferences, alternatives, and information, but we get unlucky and we get a bad result. This is the case where we make a **good decision**, but get a **bad outcome**.

Finally, and hopefully most of the time, the decision that we make is totally consistent with the preferences, alternatives, and information, and we get the results we had hoped for or better. This is the case where we make a **good decision** and get a **good outcome**. That is what this book is all about – helping you to make more "good decisions" in the belief that, in the long run, good decisions will lead to more "good outcomes."

Here are three real world examples of major decisions – what do you think about the nature of the decisions?

- Jack Welch was CEO of General Electric Corporation from 1981 to 2001. One of his more controversial ideas was to create GE University, a corporate university for training future managers. He met resistance from within and without the corporation, but Welch made the decision. He had faith in the concept, in the company, and in himself, and he stuck with that decision not knowing how it would unfold. GE's corporate university became an outstanding success, and nearly 90% of GE's top 600 managers were promoted from within the company. GE's value rose 4000 % under Welch's leadership.

- Fedex founder Fred Smith had only $5000 in the bank and a stack of bills that exceeded that amount by a considerable sum. He flew off to Las Vegas, rolled the dice (flipped the cards, pulled the lever, and who knows what else) and won $27,000 that saved the company.

- In the 1970s, Schlitz and Budweiser beers were running neck-and-neck to be the number one selling beer in America, and it was a toss-up as to which one would eventually come out on top. Each company manufactured a good product that had legions of loyal fans. The head of Schlitz Brewing Company, Robert Uihlein, Jr., decided to save money by reducing the brewing time of his company's product from 40 days to 15 days. He also decided to replace much of the barley malt used in brewing beer with much cheaper corn syrup. In addition, he made a few other decisions which had an impact on the look and taste of the beer. The decision was a profitable one – for a very short period of time. The ingredients in the new product broke down in the cans and bottles and formed something like sludge. And, according to soon-to-be Bud drinkers, the beer tasted terrible. Indecision made the company wait it out to see if matters improved. Matters didn't improve, and Schlitz had to recall 10 million cans of beer. The company never recovered.

POST-SCRIPT FROM OMAR

Not everybody knows it, but at one time I was very close to a full-time career as a recording artist and concert performer. I had made a number of very successful recordings and was even awarded two Latin Grammy Awards. A career in singing was a very real possibility for me, but I faced a serious and career make-or-break decision. Should I sign with an established record company or form my own label?

The answer should have been simple because I had already been offered a contract with one of the real powerhouses in the recording industry – Sony Music Corporation. I wanted more control over my career, however, so I turned down the contract. I still occasionally kick myself in my own can for making that decision. Running your own business is a lot of responsibility and I've never shirked responsibility in my life. But there is a learning curve in any new endeavor and that's especially true in the ever-changing and often quirky music industry. Basically, I had too much to learn in too short an amount of time to learn it. Another major factor was the need for the financing, resources, outlets and connections in many different fields essential to success. Unlike Sony, which was ideally positioned in all categories, I had none of these.

The bottom line: forming my own recording company was a bust – **bad decision, bad outcome.** I never achieved the level of success that I should have because of my lack of knowledge of the business and the lack of dollars required to support my efforts. It was, as they say, a learning experience. In some cases you can be more successful as a member of the chorus, as opposed to standing out front singing solo.

WE ARE NOT VERY GOOD AT MAKING DECISIONS

Unfortunately, as unfair as it may be, people are too often judged by the outcomes rather than by the quality of their decisions. This happens in Government, it happens in the private workplace, and it happens at home. Twenty-twenty hindsight is a wonderful thing, and it is easy to judge after-the-fact as to whether things have turned out to be good or bad. TV pundits and talking heads do it all of the time. But when you or we have to make a decision in the present, we don't have the luxury of knowing the outcome in advance. The best we can do is to make our decisions based on what we have to work with – our three pillars of preferences, alternatives, and information.

To make matters worse, the bad news is that most people really aren't very good at decision making. A colleague, Roy Gulick, used to ask people how they made decisions, and the answers were both telling and surprising. As a result of his queries, he coined the phrase, "anatomical decision making." Why anatomical? Because they would respond by saying things such as:

- "I get a *Gut* feeling."
- "I follow a rule of *Thumb.*"

- "I just think off the top of my *Head.*"

- "I usually fly by the *Seat* of my pants."

- "It is a *Knee*-jerk reaction kind of thing."

- I pulled it out of my ...."

When you boil down their responses, the common denominator is intuition. Acting on intuition is a natural part of the human condition and has a definite role in decision making. However, as the announcers say in those TV commercials – "But wait, there's more." There is a lot more to making good decisions than just following your intuition. The best outcomes are enabled by making good decisions based on the three pillars of preferences, alternatives, and information.

FOCCUSSED DECISION-MAKING

There is good news as well. There *are* steps that we can take and thought processes that we can use that go beyond intuition and that reduce the stress on all three of the challenges mentioned above. We have created an acronym to help you learn and remember the process – **FOCCUSSED**:

  Frame the problem - make sure that you are addressing the right problem and that you understand the scope of the decision.

  Objectives – know and understand the objectives and values that you want to achieve.

  Choices - develop creative, meaningful alternatives to address the decision.

  Consequences - identify the possible outcomes, good and bad, that may happen after you make the decision.

Uncertainty - think about how likely it is that events could happen that can determine the pros and cons of the future consequences.

Swaps - consider your willingness to trade one objective or consequence for another.

Solutions - once you've made a good decision, develop a plan to implement your solution.

Elicitation of data - make your decision-making processes more meaningful and productive with strong inputs to the decision.

Dissemination - communicate your decisions to others clearly and effectively.

What makes **FOCCUSSED** decision making better than some other approaches? There are many books out there that claim to have studied how people make decisions, and then describe the steps that most people follow. This is known as a descriptive approach to decision making. But, as we've pointed out earlier, we are generally bad at decision making, so these approaches present us with a process that is basically flawed from the start. The **FOCCUSSED** approach tells us how we *ought* to make decisions – it is prescriptive in nature, and therefore provides a more productive roadmap for our decision making.

The rest of this book is designed to help you become a more **FOCCUSSED** decision maker. Is the **FOCCUSSED** approach required on every decision that we make? We don't think so. One of the finest decision analysts in the world, Dr. Ralph Keeney, suggests that for every 10,000 decisions that must be made, 75% of them are "no brainers" that require little, if any, analysis. Another 5% of the decisions are really serious, very high risk, high consequence decisions that might warrant an extensive, full-scale decision analysis. [3] The remaining 20% of the decisions can be made easier and better with a **FOCCUSSED** analysis. "Which home should we purchase when we move to our retirement location and how big a mortgage should we consider?" "In which of five entrepreneurial opportunities under consideration should I invest?" "Should I start taking reduced social security payments at the earliest opportunity at age 62, or should I wait for the maximum amount at age 70?" The 20% that require a modest amount of analysis is the sweet spot for this book.

THE INTENDED AUDIENCE FOR THIS BOOK

You might ask, for whom is this book most relevant? Whether you are the CEO of a major firm, an owner or manager of a small business, a sole proprietor, or even someone who is solely focused on personal family decisions, the ideas and hints presented in this book are relevant and should help you. If you are a small business-person, you have to make decisions regarding contracts, vendors, proposals, and general operations of the firm. If you are in the financial services industry such as a realtor, insurance agent, or financial planner, you have to understand how your clients make decisions if you really want to help them. If you run a franchise such as a restaurant or fitness center, you have to make personnel decisions, equipment decisions, and financial decisions. If you are a parent, you have to make decisions about school choices, family finances, home and car purchases, etc. If you are an investor, you have to make decisions regarding when and what to buy and sell and how to manage cash flow and tax implications. Let's face it, decision making is at the heart of virtually everything we do whether we are in Government or in the private sector or just focused on our family welfare. In all cases, we have to deal with preferences, alternatives, and information. Is this book relevant to you? We are betting that it is.

This **FOCCUSSED** process leads directly to making good decisions. It is easy to understand. It is easy to follow. And that is your next decision. Are you ready to turn the page and become a more **FOCCUSSED** decision maker? What is your decision?

"While an open mind is priceless, it is only priceless when its owner has the courage to make a final decision which closes the mind for action after the process of viewing all sides of the question has been completed. Failure to make a decision after due consideration of all the facts will quickly brand a man as unfit for a position of responsibility. Not all of your decisions will be correct. None of us is perfect. But if you get into the habit of making decisions, experience will develop your judgment to a point where more and more of your decisions will be right..."

~H.W. Andrews

Chapter 2: Framing the Decision

"If you don't know where you are going,
any road will take you there."

~Lewis G. Carroll, *English author and mathematician*

The first step in the **FOCCUSSED** approach is to **F**rame the decision properly. What does that mean? It means defining the problem, identifying the constraints that limit your choices, laying out the assumptions that you are making in your analysis and, basically, setting the stage for making a quality decision. Most of us think of decision making as solving a problem. However, Ralph Keeney [4] takes a broader perspective that we really like. Don't think about decision *problems*, think about decision *opportunities*. The distinction between them may be subtle, but it is important. In solving a problem, we tend to be reactive, and this may constrain our thought process. In addressing an opportunity, we have the ability to be proactive and to possibly shape the elements of the decision in more favorable terms. In the words of President Harry S. Truman,

"A pessimist is one who makes difficulties of his opportunities, and an optimist, is one who makes opportunities of his difficulties."

When clients show us past efforts that have failed to make a winning decision, one mistake jumps out more frequently than any other. We see far too many great solutions to the wrong problems. We can't begin to tell you how many times we've been asked to look at analyses that failed, and how many times we've seen very elegant solutions to decisions that were not what the decision maker thought he or she had tasked the analysis team to look at. When the problem is improperly stated or improperly understood, the odds of getting a great solution are pretty slim.

> **Hot Tip:** *Nothing will produce a sinking feeling in the pit of your stomach faster than having a decision maker look at your recommendations and say, "That is not the problem that I asked you to solve."*

James Adams, in his book *Conceptual Blockbusting* [5] (a great and easy read, by the way), describes a problem that the agriculture industry faced years ago. The mechanical tomato pickers that were being used were damaging a high percentage of the tomato crop, having a serious impact on profits. The industry spent millions of dollars trying to solve the problem which can be paraphrased as "how can we develop a better mechanical tomato picker that will minimize damage to the crops?" After much unnecessary work, time, and money, the industry eventually solved the problem – by developing a thicker- skinned tomato! Had it initially framed the problem as "how can we keep from damaging the tomatoes during the picking process?" rather than "how can we develop a better mechanical tomato picker that will minimize damage to the crops?," a new range of alternatives would have become available for consideration much sooner, perhaps saving time and many dollars!

As an interesting diversion that is similar, years ago Japanese farmers decided to grow square watermelons to address the problem that can loosely be described as "how can we save shipping expenses and increase profits by fitting more watermelons into the shipping boxes?" They succeeded but, initially, no one would buy what were perceived as defective watermelons! What if the problem statement had been adjusted to "how can we develop watermelons *that people will buy* and that will save shipping expenses, thus increasing profits by fitting more watermelons into the shipping boxes?" The added phrase may well have affected their marketing efforts. They eventually solved the problem. Today, farmers grow and sell square watermelons (by growing them in a square container) that are smaller in size and are designed to fit into the smaller refrigerators owned by most Japanese citizens. However, they are inedible since they are picked before they are ripe – the Japanese use them for decorations rather than for food. You can buy them for around $80 apiece and, in Russia, they were recently selling for more than $800 apiece!

Fortunately, there are some really good tools available to us to help frame decisions that are relatively easy to use. The first thing we should do is ask *"why."* Many people, when faced with a difficult decision, start by talking about "what" they should do and "how" should they do it. It is far better to start with "why" which includes the *purpose of the decision, the viewpoints* from which the decision should be judged, and *the constraints and boundaries* on the decision. Sometimes, the purpose is to correct something about the status quo that has changed or gone wrong – something has deviated from business as usual. On other occasions, the status quo is acceptable, but new opportunities present themselves on the horizon. As for viewpoint, for many entrepreneurs, each is the sole decision maker whose perspective should be considered but, for others, there may be additional stakeholders such as a spouse, business partner, investor, or even the providers of services that the decision maker may have to rely upon such as a bank for a business loan.

PROBLEM ANALYSIS

Let's take a quick look at how we might approach the situation when something has moved away from what seems normal, usually for the worse. In those situations, we find ourselves in the role of a diagnostician. Interestingly enough, that role is basically the same whether we are doctors looking at symptoms trying to determine the disease causing them, intelligence analysts looking at indicators of what the bad guys are doing and trying to ascertain if there is malevolent intent, or stockbrokers who chart the market closely and are trying to determine what caused a 1000 point drop in the Dow Jones Average in a week. This diagnostic process goes by a variety of names to include problem analysis, differential diagnosis, root-cause analysis, and analysis of competing hypotheses.

Charles Kepner and Benjamin Tregoe, in their book, *The New Rational Manager* [6], call this **problem analysis** and it has five steps:

1. **Clearly state the nature of the deviation** – state what has happened that differs from the usual.

2. **Identify the details of the deviation** – describe what is happening in terms of what you are seeing or hearing that you shouldn't be, as well as things that you are *not* seeing or hearing that you should be.

3. **Develop possible causes of the deviation** – List as many possible causes of the deviation as you can without judging them.

4. **Test for the most possible cause** – Take each possible cause, one at a time, and identify whether the details of the deviation are consistent with that being the cause of the problem. Then narrow the possible causes down to the one or two that are most consistent with what is happening.

5. **Verify the true cause** – Take one action at a time to eliminate the cause until the deviation disappears.

We'll illustrate with an example from Terry's recent air conditioning experience. He and his wife noticed that their home in Florida was exceptionally hot. Of course, it was 96° outside, but this was definitely not right. The thermostat in the master bedroom was set at 74° but read 89°, the thermostat near the laundry room was set at 74° but read 80°, and the thermostat near the rec room (which was an addition to the house) was set at 74° but read 75°. It didn't take a rocket scientist to recognize that the cooling system was not operating properly (no offense intended to the readers who are rocket scientists). Being a trained decision analyst, and having studied Kepner-Tregoe, Terry began to triage the problem. His wife laughed and suggested that they just call the air conditioning repairman and pay whatever it takes for an emergency call on a weekend. Terry ignored her affront to his abilities as the man of the house to be Mr. Fix-It and continued his assessment of the situation.

Nature of the deviation: The house was roasting regardless of where he set the thermostats when, normally, it is cool and comfortable.

Details of the deviation: They first noticed warmer temperatures the day before, but shrugged it off due to exceptionally hot weather, especially since they hadn't noticed it before then. They had been having some power surges over the last few days, but only for a few seconds with no major outages. Most of the house was hot except for the rec room, which was cool and on its own air conditioning unit. The fans were running in all three air conditioning units, but the compressor outside was only spinning for the rec room unit.

Possible causes of the deviation: Not knowing much about air conditioning, Terry thought of the obvious. One or more of the compressors could have failed, circuit breakers could have blown or become defective, surge protectors in the units could have turned the units off during power surges, Freon levels could be low, thereby causing ineffective operations, or the thermostats could have been defective, thus sending the wrong signals to the units.

Test for the most possible cause: The circuit breakers in the garage appeared to be working since, when Terry tripped each one, the fan in the associated unit stopped spinning. The units were clearly getting electricity. The compressor for the rec room was spinning, the one for the laundry room area was not spinning, but the unit was hot to the touch which indicated that it had been operational, and the unit for the master bedroom wasn't moving at all and was cool to the touch. The thermostats had operated properly previously, but he had no way to test whether they were operational other than changing their batteries. At this point, Terry was confident that the most likely cause was damage to the master bedroom unit, and possibly the laundry room unit, caused by power surges.

Verify true cause: The Kepner-Tregoe approach had allowed Terry to hone in on the most likely cause of the problem. But since he had exhausted his knowledge of air conditioning repairs, he was unable to take many of the physical steps to verify the true cause. He proudly declared to his wife that it was now time to call the professional repairman to fix the problem, and the repairman showed up within an hour. The repairman confirmed Terry's hypothesis when he visually checked the thermostats, tested the circuit breakers (both the ones in the garage that Terry had tested and the ones outside that Terry didn't know how to access), ran some diagnostics, and determined that an internal surge protector in the compressor for the master bedroom had blown and needed to be replaced, most likely as a result of the power surge. Not only that, he found that the internal surge protector in the unit for the laundry room was also defective and needed to be replaced. Two units gone at the same time! Within 30 minutes (much to the glee of Terry's wife who stared at him with that smug "I told you so" look that only a wife can muster), both surge protectors were replaced and the problem was solved.

Terry's air conditioner failure was a pretty straightforward and well defined problem. Unfortunately, in most cases, even when we understand what is going wrong, we still have a lot of work to do in order to decide what actions we should take. Setting the stage for identifying those actions is the hard part.

CASE STUDY: MIKE AND MADDIE ROSE – FRAMING THE PROBLEM

As we continue to explore **FOCCUSSED** decision making, we'll use the case of Mike and Maddie Rose to illustrate the key concepts:

Mike and Maddie are in their thirties, live in Boca Raton, Florida, and have two small children. Maddie is a stay-at-home mom. Mike works in a relatively low-paying job and, while they are able to make ends meet each month, they are not saving as much as they need to for the future. Mike is not particularly happy in his job, and has always wanted to be in charge of his own company. Mike has two passions – he loves to cook and he is an avid fitness buff who works out six days a week. Each day, he hears many radio ads for franchising opportunities in several different industries. After a particularly depressing day at work, he hears of a small restaurant chain that is looking for entrepreneurs to train. He comes home and tells Maddie "I'm seriously considering leaving my job and taking a franchise in the restaurant business. There's an opportunity that is close to where we live, and I think we have the opportunity to raise our standard of living. What do you think?" Maddie replies, "You've been talking about something like this for a while, and I'll support whatever you want to do. But I know you've also been talking about getting into the fitness business and you might be happier there. Why limit the decision to a restaurant franchise?" After thinking about it, Mike realizes that Maddie is right; why should they limit their opportunities to a single choice. In the restaurant opportunity, he would be the manager and would be putting in very long hours since he'd have to be on the premises most of the time. With fitness franchises, he'd have more choices. Mike could be a hands-on manager, or else he could be an owner/investor and hire someone else to do the day-to-day management chores. Mike tells Maddie that "I was looking at the restaurant alternative from the perspective of it being close to the house, and we wouldn't have to disrupt you and the kids very much. However, the fitness clubs that seem to be available might require that we move, or I'll be commuting for hours each day which I don't want to do." Maddie leaps at the opportunity. "Mike, you know that I've felt that this house was getting too small for us and, since we've talked about having more children, I'd welcome the chance to move into a bigger house and raise our standard of living. I have no problem moving to an area that works for you if you take a franchising chance." Mike becomes elated that he is no longer constrained by his current location and, as a result, his set of choices for a new start has grown greatly. By framing the decision in terms of the needs of the "stakeholders" (Mike, Maddie, and the kids), Mike has managed to more clearly define the frame of the decision that he is facing. Now, instead of addressing the problem of "Should I consider leaving my current job to take a franchise in the restaurant business near my home?," he can think in terms of "Should I consider leaving my current job for a franchising opportunity in either the restaurant business or the fitness center business that will enable us to raise our standard of living?" By more clearly articulating the decision frame, Mike and Maddie are better positioned to make a decision that addresses the real, expanded opportunity.

Case Study: The Frequent Flier – Framing the Problem

We are firm believers that the best way to learn something is to practice it, so let's see how you do at framing a problem that was motivated by a recent experience of Omar's (with some poetic license on our part). He was taking a trip to the Caribbean for a long weekend of scuba diving and had the following encounter at the airport ticket counter. He was told that two of his bags, for which he had already paid $25 per bag online to check, were each five pounds overweight for the international flight at a penalty of $200 apiece. The counter attendant posed a straightforward decision problem for him – "Sir, which credit card would you like to use for the excess baggage fees?"

Take a few minutes to frame Omar's decision problem before looking at the next paragraph.

If you took the simple approach, you basically re-stated the question that was facing him as "which credit card should I use to pay for the excess baggage fees?" Some of you might have thought that Omar's decision was "how can I eliminate the $200 in excess baggage fees?" and suggested to him that he get out of line, go to the outside baggage drop point, and "tip" the Skycap $25 in the hope that he'd overlook the weight issue. Some of you might have suggested that Omar's decision is "how can I repack my checked bags to eliminate all or part of the excess baggage fees?" Now, Terry admits that on some winter trips from Florida to the Northeast, he had run into a similar problem and quickly pulled a sweater and winter coat out of his bag to reduce the weight and wore them onto the plane even though it was 85° outside. But, we doubt that Omar would consider taking off his flip flops and putting on his heavier snorkeling flippers to walk onto the plane. In actuality, Omar was a savvy traveler and framed his question as "how can I get the most value for the fees that I am paying?" Omar ignored what appeared to be the initial constraints of the situation and asked the counter attendant what the cost would be for a last-minute First Class upgrade for a premier-level traveler who flew more than 100,000 miles per year on that airline. Omar was told that for $175, he could upgrade to First Class, and the upgrade would include an increased weight allowance, two-free checked bags, early boarding, and the usual amenities of a First Class seat. Clearly, Omar had shaped the decision by framing it in the best way possible.

ARTICULATING THE VISION

One tool that we've found to be very helpful in problem framing is the **vision statement** that incorporates these three key questions:

- Why are we doing this?
- What should we do?
- How will we know that we have succeeded in the decision?

The first two questions are relatively easy, but the third one is often misapplied. Our natural tendency is to judge the quality of our decision by the ultimate outcome. For example, if a person makes a decision to change jobs, it is tempting to say the decision will be successful if, within a year, he triples his salary and gets promoted to a management position. The problem in thinking that way is that the success criteria indicated above won't be known at the time of the decision - they represent after-the-fact assessments of whether he made a good decision (remember the difference between a good decision and a good outcome!). In the third question, we have to focus on the nature of the decision, not on the future outcome.

To illustrate a vision statement, let's continue looking in on Mike and Maddie. Their vision statement might look like this:

Why are we making the decision? – Mike is unhappy in his work, and is not earning enough. The timing is right from a family standpoint to make a change that will better its standard of living. Several opportunities have presented themselves that may improve Mike's situation.

What should we do? – After discussions with Maddie, it is decided that Mike should look at franchising opportunities in both the restaurant industry and the fitness industry. They are willing to move to take advantage of the right opportunity.

How will we know when we have succeeded (in the decision)? – Mike and Maddie will have succeeded when they have been able to identify a franchising alternative that meets their most important objectives, is consistent with their financial situation and risk tolerance levels, and has a distinct advantage over the other alternatives.

IDENTIFYING KEY ISSUES AND STAKEHOLDERS

With the vision statement guiding the way, the next step in our framing process is to identify the key issues that must be considered in making the decision. Most issues will fall into one of three categories. Some of these issues will directly relate to the **choices** that we have. Others will relate to our knowledge or lack of knowledge – that is, **our state of information**, or **key uncertainties.** Still other issues are related to how we will **measure the degree of satisfaction** of our objectives and values by the alternatives.

Issues can fall into many areas including financial or economic, legal, technological, organizational, cultural, emotional, etc. A nice way to represent what we are facing is with a Stakeholder Issue

Identification Matrix. We list the types of issues as rows in the matrix, the stakeholders as columns, and in the body of the matrix, we identify the specific issue. An abbreviated Stakeholder Issue Identification Matrix for Mike and Maddie might look like the following:

Issues	Decision Maker/Stakeholders			
	Mike	Maddie	Franchisor	Bank
Financial	Net income	Net income	Mike's finances	Mike's finances
	Initial investment	Impact on savings	Collateral	Interest rates
Economic	Competition		Location availability	The economy
			Impact of other franchisees	
	Availability of qualified staff			
Social		Leaving friends		
		Change kids' schools		
Organizational			Mike's skill set	
	Management role - hands on?		Mike's managerial commitment	
Legal	Type of corporation			Type of corporation

The Stakeholder Issue Identification Matrix is useful in that it helps to make sure that we are including the important aspects of the decision and that we are solving the right problem. It doesn't, by itself, help us to select the best alternative.

The Decision Hierarchy

There is one other concept worth mentioning that can help us to frame the problem properly. In the *Handbook of Decision Analysis* [7], that Terry co-authored, we talk about a decision hierarchy. It is easy to get wrapped up in past decisions and future decisions that are associated with the opportunity that we are facing, and the decision hierarchy helps to hone in on the core of the decision at hand. We categorize the decision possibilities into three bins:

1. Decisions that have already been made and are taken as "givens"

2. Decisions that are the ones that we currently face

3. Decisions that we will make later

For all practical purposes, #1 and #3 are outside of the scope of the decision that we are currently facing, and we can avoid dealing with them now. As an example, we can create the following decision hierarchy for Mike and Maddie:

1. **Decisions that have already been made and are taken as "givens" :**

    - Mike plans on changing jobs to improve their standard of living

    - Job change opportunities have been narrowed to franchises in either the restaurant or fitness industries

    - Moving to a different location is acceptable to both of them.

2. **Decisions that Mike and Maddie currently face:**

    - Which type of franchise should Mike select?

- Which specific franchise will best meet their objectives?

3. **Decisions that Mike and Maddie will make later:**
   - Should they move?
   - If so, where and which house?
   - How will Mike operate the selected franchise?

With their decision well-framed and all of the issues identified, Mike and Maddie are now ready to start identifying and evaluating their objectives and specific choices.

RAPID RECAP: FRAMING THE DECISION

- Framing the decision means defining the problem, identifying the constraints that limit your choices, laying out the assumptions that you are making in your analysis and, basically, setting the stage for making a quality decision.

- Many people, when faced with a difficult decision, start by talking about "what" they should do and "how" they should do it. It is better to start with "why" which includes the *purpose of the decision, the viewpoints* from which the decision should be judged, and *the constraints and boundaries* on the decision.

- A **vision statement** for the decision incorporates the three key questions:
  - Why are we doing this?
  - What should we do?

o How will we know that we have succeeded in the decision?

- A Stakeholder Issue Identification Matrix is useful in helping us to make sure that we are including the important aspects of the decision and that we are solving the right problem. It doesn't, by itself, help us to select the best alternative.

- A decision hierarchy helps to hone in on the core of the decision at hand by categorizing the decision possibilities into three bins:

    o Decisions that have already been made and are taken as "givens"

    o Decisions that are the ones that we currently face

    o Decisions that we will make later.

"When you come to a fork in the road, take it."

~Yogi Berra, *Great American Philosopher*

NOTES:

Chapter 3: Understanding Objectives and Values

"The greater danger for most of us lies not in setting our aim too high and falling short; but in setting our aim too low, and achieving our mark."

~Michelangelo, *Italian artist and poet*

When you really get down to it, decision making is all about achieving the objectives that reflect our values and preferences.

Hot Tip: *There is no such thing as a "right" decision that applies to everyone or, at least, we've never come across one. When it comes to what makes a "good decision," one size does not fit all.*

The best car for you if you mostly do city driving may not be the best car for your brother if he is constantly on the road for great distances calling on clients. Some folks wouldn't buy a home in Florida without a pool because they love a morning swim, but there are others who wouldn't buy a home *with* a pool because they worry about the safety of small children. In this chapter, we'll explore the notion of objectives and values, and teach you how to better incorporate them in your decision-making efforts.

Value-Focused Thinking: Understanding Objectives and Values

In Chapter 2, we learned how to frame our decision opportunity properly. We call the next step in our **FOCCUSSED** decision-making approach "**O**bjectives," and by that we mean understanding the objectives and values that you hope to achieve through your decision. Many people, when faced with a difficult decision, start by identifying a set of alternatives that they will consider, and then figuring out what criteria they will use to decide among the alternatives. This is known as alternatives-focused thinking (AFT). It is very common and is the reverse of how we *should* make decisions.

Ralph Keeney is credited with developing a different and better approach known as value-focused thinking, or VFT [8]. In VFT, we start with the objectives and values that we are trying to satisfy *before* identifying the alternatives. By doing this, we are in a better position to be proactive in shaping our decision opportunities to maximize potential value for those with a stake in the decision. Once we've identified these objectives and values, we then use them to develop more creative alternatives and to later evaluate and improve those alternatives or to develop new ones. There are many advantages to the VFT approach including helping us to shape decisions rather than to react to them, identifying objectives that may not be immediately obvious, focusing our information collection efforts, capturing conflicting perspectives, and improving communications.

In the world of large corporations, we often find that the primary objective of any decision is improving **shareholder value**. The focus is on balance sheets, income statements, Net Present Value, and Returns on Investment (ROIs). While these types of major corporate decisions are important and require exceptional decision skills, as indicated earlier, they are not the focus of this book. We are more interested in **stakeholder value** than shareholder value, whether the decision involves a single stakeholder (you) or multiple stakeholders (you and a spouse, investors, financiers, etc.). What makes things interesting is that, often, the objectives of the stakeholders are not aligned and may even be in direct conflict. One only has to look at some of the major decisions facing Congress these days and it is plain to see that, on virtually every major decision, the objectives of the Republicans and the Democrats seem to differ and are at odds. But this is the reality of making tough decisions – where you stand depends on where you sit. Objectives and values are not universal.

Let's focus our attention for now on the more straightforward cases of a single decision maker such as many of you, or of a couple making family-oriented decisions together. How do we do a good job of clearly identifying the objectives that should drive a decision? Recall that in framing the problem, one of the key questions to ask is "Why are we making this decision?" Keeney coined the term **fundamental objectives** to represent the most basic values that we are trying to achieve. For example, in selecting a career choice, the fundamental objective may be "select a career that will allow me to retire at age 55 without having to compromise my standard of living." In making an insurance-related decision, it may be "provide a means of taking care of my wife and children financially after I die so that they will never have to worry about finances." Fundamental objectives typically answer the question of "why am I making the decision?" There doesn't necessarily have to be a *single* fundamental objective in a decision. We can break it into fundamental sub-objectives if that helps us to think about the decision more easily.

Compare fundamental objectives to what Keeney calls **means objectives**. Means objectives describe the way that we can accomplish fundamental objectives. For example, if one of our fundamental objectives in buying a car is to procure a vehicle that "provides the maximum levels of safety for occupants of the vehicle," the means objectives may include "maximize the number of air bags," "reduce side collisions via blind spot monitoring," and "reduce front end collisions via collision detection and prevention sensors." Means objectives typically answer the question of "*how* can I best achieve my fundamental objective?"

Why do we need to distinguish between fundamental objectives and means objectives? As we get further into our **FOCCUSSED** process, we will be using our fundamental objectives to evaluate the alternatives. Most people get overwhelmed in making decisions by getting lost in the means objectives. If we are too focused on the means objectives, the evaluation will be more complicated and less efficient, and we won't be able to "see the forest for the trees." If we instead focus on the fundamental objectives, we can capture the really important distinctions among the alternatives in a far more efficient and meaningful manner. In our car example, a fundamental objective might be to provide enough rapid acceleration to pass cars safely and save lives on high speed highways (the "why"). A means objective might be to purchase a car with an 8-cylinder, high performance engine (the "how"). There is an important difference between how an alternative *performs* on an evaluation criteria and how strongly we *value or prefer* that level of performance. Means objectives help us to understand the nature of our choices and how they will perform, but it is the fundamental objectives that tell us what that level of performance is worth to us. More on this important topic is to come later.

One way of distinguishing a means objective from a fundamental objective is the "why test." Ask why you have included a specific objective to evaluate your alternatives. If you can provide a good answer to the why question, you probably aren't talking about a fundamental objective. For example, when a person asks "why do I want an 8-cylinder, high performance engine?" the answer probably is "to provide enough rapid acceleration to pass cars safely and save lives on high speed highways." When the person asks the question "why do I want to pass cars safely and save lives on high speed highways?" the answer is so basic that a higher-level reason can't be provided. The answer may be "just because!" That tells us that we have identified a fundamental objective!

Screening Criteria

Now that we understand why objectives are important, how do we go about determining and organizing the objectives that we will use in our decision? The first step is to determine what objectives are absolutely must haves and are non-negotiable. We call those **screening criteria**. For example, when Terry bought his last car, before he started to look at specific cars, he determined that the final choice had to provide access through four doors, seat at least five, provide a positioning/locating system that was factory installed, and that would allow his 4' 10" wife to see over the steering wheel easily (harder to find than you would think). Any car that didn't meet all of these objectives wouldn't be considered, no matter how well it met his other objectives. Think of screening criteria as being mandatory and they can't be traded off for other features.

How Can We Identify Objectives?

The next step is to identify the objectives that can be prioritized and traded-off with each other. It is not always an easy task to develop a good set of objectives, and we frequently forget to include some very important objectives. One approach to discovering objectives is to go through a brainstorming exercise in which we ask ourselves a series of probing questions, the answers to which may help to reveal our true objectives. These questions to ask yourself might include:

- How would I describe the characteristics of a really great alternative?

- How would I describe the characteristics of a really terrible alternative?

- If money were no object, what would I do?

- If I were my competition, what would I want to happen?

- What is great about my current situation?

- What is wrong with my current situation?

The answers to these questions will likely be redundant, unorganized, and disconnected, but with a little effort we can group them, organize them, and reword them to form the basis for our objectives.

When we talk about trade-offs, we mean the ability to get more satisfaction of one objective at the expense of another. In our car example, the need for more acceleration capability for high-speed passing may work against trying to minimize fuel costs. Our goal is to identify enough objectives to be able to say that our evaluation captures most of what is important, but not too many that will result in overlap and create an evaluation nightmare. All too often, people try to capture every possible aspect of the decision, and that can be overwhelming. We are firm believers in what is known as **Pareto's Rule** named after Italian economist, Vilfredo Pareto. [9] It is also known as the 80-20 rule, and it says that roughly 80% of effects come from 20% of the causes.

Hot Tip: *Typically, 20% of clients cause 80% of the aggravation and 20% of clients account for 80% of net income (but, fortunately, it is not the same 20 %!).*

In decision making, 20% of the objectives usually account for 80% of the value that we are trying to achieve. The name of the game is to identify the objectives that are the most important to us and initially ignore the remaining 80% of them. This is critical - one of the hardest things for people to do is to know when to stop analyzing things. In the words of the great Albert Einstein,

*"Everything should be made as simple as possible,
but not simpler."*

Additionally, the set of objectives needs to be reliable and understandable so that there is no confusion as to what an objective means – good definitions are critical. Most importantly, the set of objectives must be able to differentiate effectively among the alternatives.

CASE STUDY: STRATEGIC PLANNER WENDI LEE – IDENTIFYING OBJECTIVES

Let's see how we can operationalize these concepts. Wendi Lee, a strategic planner, has determined that her current Dell PC Laptop is no longer operating efficiently and needs to be replaced. Her fundamental objective for the replacement system is to provide mobile computing capability for the suite of application software that she regularly uses with her clients. Notice that in framing the fundamental objective, Wendi did not say "provide a replacement PC laptop" – after all, these days, she might be able to get the capability she needs from a Mac, from a tablet, or perhaps even from a smart phone. It gets back to focusing on the "why" and not the "how" of the decision. By defining the objective in terms of function or capability rather than components, her range of alternatives is expanded. Next, she identifies her screening criteria. Since she travels by air a lot and has to carry the device, she will not accept a solution that weighs more than three pounds. Since she does many presentations from her device, she must have a system that can display simultaneously on both an external projector and on her screen. Since she uses many applications that were designed for a Microsoft Windows environment, the solution must include the capability to run

Windows-based applications. Finally, since she has several other asset purchases to make, she sets her maximum budget for acquisition at $4,000 to include the basic software packages she would need to become operational (pretty high for a mobile device these days).

With her screening criteria identified, she can begin to identify what is called an objectives hierarchy. The objectives hierarchy is just an outline framework for representing her objectives. She can break her fundamental objective into lower-level objectives such as "maximize effective computing capability" and "minimize life-cycle costs." If these were well defined enough, she could stop here and go no further, but she believes that these are too high level and not specific enough. After giving it a lot of thought, she's come up with a value hierarchy that meets the 80-20 rule and that will enable her to distinguish among the eventual alternatives that she will consider. What is noteworthy here is that by using value-focused thinking, Wendi did not need to know the alternatives before developing the hierarchy! Wendi has developed her hierarchy of objectives as shown below:

Fundamental Objective: Provide the capability for mobile computing that can accommodate the suite of application software regularly used with clients.

Maximize effective computing capability

1. Maximize computing performance levels

    o Provide sufficient processing capability to run graphics -intensive applications, mathematical simulation applications, and database queries

    o Provide a minimum of 128 Gigabytes of internal storage with capability for adding external storage devices

    o Provide an extremely high resolution display

2. Provide for interface with numerous devices

   o Provide capability for wireless connectivity

   o Provide capability for hard-wired Ethernet capability

   o Provide for both read/write record and play capabilities

   o Provide capability with all connectors currently in use (e.g., USB, HDMI, mini-HDMI)

3. Provide systems characteristics that meet mobile computing needs

   o Minimize carrying weight to include peripherals and cords

   o Maximize battery life

   o Provide durability required for heavy travel use

   o Provide availability of an on-site 24/7 repair and servicing capability

Minimize life-cycle costs

4. Minimize acquisition cost (maximum of $4,000)

5. Minimize maintenance and repair costs (e.g., warranties)

At this point in her mobile computing decision (remember, it is not simply a "laptop" purchase decision), Wendi has organized the objectives needed to select a great alternative. But she hasn't yet shown how she is going to measure the "goodness" or "badness" of her alternatives. She does this by next defining what are known as value measures, or metrics, that she can use to judge her choices. In essence, a value measure describes what is meant by good or bad performance and, later, can be used to compare alternatives. She needs at least one value measure for each objective at the lowest level of her hierarchy – that is, in the outline framework shown above, the bullets that are furthest to the right in each section of the outline. For example, for the objective of "maximize battery life," her value measure might be the number of hours that she can operate without being connected to an external power source. For the objective of "provide a minimum of 128 Gigabytes of internal storage with capability for adding external storage devices," she might want more than one value measure. More is better, so one value measure might be bytes of internal storage provided. She can also get more storage by interfacing with an external drive, so another value measure might be the ability to interface with an unlimited size external hard drive.

In this step of the process, Wendi is simply defining in words the measures of satisfaction for her objectives. She still has to develop scales that she can use for the actual measurements (and this will be covered in a later chapter).

CASE STUDY: BUYING A HOUSE – DEVELOPING OBJECTIVES

Now it is time for you to practice. Let's say you are buying a new house in the same town where you live. Without looking at the next paragraph, take a few minutes to jot down the top 10 or so objectives that the house you choose should satisfy. Include any screening criteria that you might have. Don't worry about the value measures for now.

There is no right or wrong answer to this exercise, but as an example of things to consider, when Terry and his wife, Andrea, made their last move to Boca Raton, Florida, their top objectives included the following, along with the "why" aspect:

Screening criteria (must haves):

1. Cost no more than 10% above the price at which they had just sold their house in Virginia (resources for down payment were constrained).

2. Must be in a specified high school district (they had already identified the two choices for schools that their youngest daughter might attend, one public, and one private).

3. Provide at least three bedrooms and an office space (Terry's mother-in-law would be living with them).

4. Everything must be on one level with no steps, not even a sunken living room (too many klutzes in the family; steps, even small ones, definitely would lead to disaster).

Objectives that can be traded-off:

5. Provide easy access to both Palm Beach and Ft. Lauderdale airports (Terry was commuting to Washington D.C. every week).

6. Have a gourmet kitchen with separate breakfast area (Andrea loves to cook, Terry loves to eat).

7. Have a pool (Terry would be retiring soon and wanted a place to relax in the sun).

8. Have at least a two-car garage (it's too hot to keep cars outside in Florida).

9. Have adequate living room/dining room to entertain large groups (they love to entertain!).

10. Have a great view (when they look out their windows, they want to say "wow!").

11. Be in a development with nice community amenities such as tennis, club house, and exercise facility, but no need for a golf course (they like to be part of a community).

They actually used this list to develop a score sheet for the houses that they looked at, and they couldn't be happier with the house that they picked.

CASE STUDY: MIKE AND MADDIE – DEVELOPING OBJECTIVES

To bring the concepts of this chapter together, let's get back to Mike and Maddie and see how they are doing in their decision process.

As part of framing the problem and identifying issues, Mike performed extensive research and has spoken to other franchise owners. As a result, he has decided to limit his search to franchises in the fitness industry since that is where his passion really lies. More than 40 million Americans are members of health clubs, the overall industry generates more than $10 billion each year, and these numbers are growing. Whereas the industry used to focus on 18-34 year-olds, its popularity has spread over all age groups. Mike has learned that some of the opportunities are narrowly focused such as those that cater to women, focus on group training, provide "boot camp" training, or strictly attract seniors. However, there are others with a wider focus on broad-based health rather than just fitness. Many smaller franchises are "basic gym" oriented, while major players such as L.A. Fitness often have full-scope programs including basketball and racquetball courts, swimming pools, babysitting, health bars, and even restaurants. Some franchises allow franchisees with as little as $50,000 in net worth and $70,000 in liquid cash available, while others might require as much as $1.5 million in net worth and $400,000 in liquid cash available. Some franchises have lease terms of as little as three years, while others could go on as long as 10 years.

As Mike started to think about why he was considering a job change, his fundamental objective became clear:

Mike's fundamental objective: Raise our standard of living by finding a fitness industry franchise that will provide long-term growth, stability, and a job that I am passionate about, and that will also allow me more quality time with my family.

As he started to flesh out his objectives hierarchy, Mike brainstormed the issues that he needed to consider. There were so many of them initially that he was quickly overwhelmed. Some of the questions that came to mind included:

- Do I want to focus on fitness, or think bigger in terms of health?

- Can I find a location that meets my family's needs yet will bring in the kind of business that I'll need to grow the franchise?

- What kind of compensation package is there for me in the short term?

- What is the long-term potential for creating wealth for my family?

- Do I want to start with a small opportunity with a narrow focus, or do I go big right from the start?

- Which opportunities are consistent with my net worth and available cash?

- How affordable are the opportunities both in terms of initial investment cost and ongoing expenses?

- Does the franchise chain have a track record of success within the fitness and health industry and within the franchising industry in general?

- What kind of competition will I be facing?

- How much support will I get from the franchise, or am I basically on my own for all support such as accounting, equipment, and marketing?

- How easy will it be to find qualified employees?

- How well will the franchise train me since I've never done this before?

At this point, Mike's head was spinning. Fortunately, Mike knew about the 80-20 rule, and he began to identify his screening criteria:

- Eliminate franchises with very narrowly focused client-bases such as boot-camps, single-gender, or limited age-group audiences

- Eliminate franchises that provide no third-party support whatsoever for things such as accounting, training, and equipment maintenance

- Eliminate franchises that require investments well in excess of our current financial situation

- Eliminate franchises that are poorly rated by Franchise 500, a well-known franchise rating service.

Next, he started to organize his thoughts in terms of what he thought really mattered the most. Eventually, he felt pretty comfortable that his objectives and value measures could best be represented as:

Maximize long-term wealth from franchise ownership

- Maximize the track record of success

  o Measured by average annual profits of other owners within the same franchise

  o Measured by Franchise 500 ranking

  o Measured by projected cash flows

- Maximize opportunities for membership growth

  o Minimize competition

    ▪ Measured by distance from nearest same-franchise competition

    ▪ Measured by number of competing fitness franchises in the area he is considering

  o Maximize the ability to offer affordable memberships

    ▪ Measured by incentives offered by the franchise chains

    ▪ Measured by the profit margins that are acceptable

  o Maximize the quality of the equipment

    ▪ Measured by the state-of-the art of the equipment that the franchise will provide

    ▪ Measured by the quantity and variety of equipment available on the open market.

Maximize the enjoyment of the franchisee experience

- Provide a franchise that will be enjoyable to own and operate

  o Maximize third-party support provided

    ▪ Measured by the breadth and affordability of third-party services provided (e.g., accounting, marketing, etc.)

    ▪ Measured by the projected quality of third-party services provided

  o Maximize the opportunity to attract qualified staff

    ▪ Measured by the ability to retain existing staff if at an existing franchise

    ▪ Measured by the availability of quality staff if at a new franchise

    ▪ Measured by the ability to offer competitive compensation packages including benefits provided by the franchise chain.

- Maximize time spent with family without sacrificing performance

  o Maximize flexibility in managing the franchise

    ▪ Measured by average hours spent at the facility each day by franchisees at other same-chain locations

  o Minimize daily commuting time

    ▪ Measured by availability of affordable housing a short commuting distance from the franchise.

Provide an economically viable business opportunity

- Minimize difference between owner's net worth/liquid cash available and franchise's required net worth/liquid cash available

    o Measured by Mike's net worth and liquid cash available

    o Measured by Mike's ability to obtain affordable financing

- Optimize investment costs

    o Minimize initial capital contribution/franchise fee

        ▪ Measured by required initial capital contribution/ franchise fee

    o Minimize annual royalty fees

        ▪ Measured by required royalty fees

    o Minimize annual operating costs

        ▪ Measured by average recurring operating costs of same-chain franchises

    o Minimize annual equipment replacement costs

        ▪ Measured by average annual equipment replacement costs of same-chain franchises

- Maximize long-term job stability

    o Maximize the length of franchising agreement

        ▪ Measured by the length of the franchise agreement.

With their objectives clearly stated, Mike and Maddie are confident that they will be able to select a great alternative for Mike's franchise.

Next, it is time to identify a workable set of alternatives that they can evaluate.

RAPID RECAP: UNDERSTANDING OBJECTIVES AND VALUES

- Decision making is all about achieving the objectives that reflect our values and preferences.

- There is no such thing as a "right" decision that applies to everyone.

- Many people use alternative-focused thinking (AFT) to make decisions. A far better approach is to use value-focused thinking (VFT) in which we start with the objectives and values that we are trying to satisfy before identifying the alternatives.

- **Fundamental objectives** represent the most basic values that we are trying to achieve and answer the question "why?" **Means objectives** describe the way that we can accomplish those fundamental objectives and answer the question "how?" In making decisions, our primary focus should be on the fundamental objectives.

- **Screening criteria** are mandatory and they can't be traded off for other features. They are absolutely must haves and are non-negotiable.

- Remember **Pareto's Rule** also known as the 80-20 rule. In decision making, 20% of the objectives usually account for 80% of the value.

- We use an **objectives hierarchy** as a framework to represent the objectives that can be prioritized and traded-off with each other. The objectives need to be complete, non-overlapping, reliable, understandable and, most importantly, must differentiate effectively among the alternatives.

- We use **value measures** to describe what is meant by good or bad performance and, later, to compare our alternatives. We need at least one value measure for each objective at the lowest level of our hierarchy.

"Our age is characterized by the perfection of means and the confusion of goals."

~Albert Einstein

NOTES:

Chapter 4: Creating Choices

"The problem, simply put, is that we cannot choose everything simultaneously. So we live in danger of becoming paralyzed by indecision, terrified that every choice might be the wrong choice."

~Elizabeth Gilbert, *Committed: A Skeptic Makes Peace with Marriage*

We've talked about making sure that we are solving the right problem and about our objectives which represent the things that we value. The next step in **FOCCUSSED** decision making is to develop the Choices that are available to us. Whether they are called choices, options, alternatives, courses of action, or something else, they are the elements of a decision over which we have control. We get to define the set of choices that we want to evaluate in a way that best meets our objectives and values.

That said, there are circumstances in which we don't have the luxury of thoughtful analysis of possible choices. Think of military leaders in the heat of combat, emergency first responders who need to act in the blink of an eye, or emergency room doctors who must make split-second life-or-death decisions. In these types of situations, rather than engaging in time consuming analysis, they make instant choices based on training and instinct. They recognize a situation as something they've seen in training or in their experience, and instinctively select the right course of action without much deliberation. The "decision maker" in such circumstances quickly considers an alternative, assesses whether it fits the situation, and accepts the first one that appears to work. Gary Klein refers to this as **recognition-primed decision making**. [10]

In most situations, most of us are not under those types of time constraints in the decisions that we face. We have the luxury of time and the ability to consider more carefully multiple choices and to perform a thoughtful analysis.

In its simplest form, we can generate a choice, compare it to our objectives, and decide if it is "good enough." If it is, we don't consider additional choices. If it is not, we generate another choice and continue the process until we pass the "good enough" test. This approach is known as **satisficing** and was developed by Herbert Simon in 1956. [11] Satisficing is a decision-making strategy that entails searching through the available choices until we find one that clears our threshold. We can compare this with the **FOCCUSSED** approach to decision making that attempts to find the *best* alternative available. For most of us, *good enough* isn't acceptable and we prefer to make an optimal decision.

Developing Better Choices

It is hard to make an optimal decision if all of our choices are bad choices. Yes, we can select the "best of the bad" but, if we really want to make a good decision, we need to develop a good set of alternatives. In some cases, the alternatives are many and easy to find. For example, a realtor helping her client buy a new home can search the multiple listings to produce many choices that fit the client's objectives. A financial planner can look at *Morningstar* or *Moody's Ratings* to produce a long list of viable investment choices. A potential franchisee can simply google "franchises available in my zip code" to produce a diverse set of opportunities. But for many decisions, the alternatives are not as obvious, and we need to do some creative thinking to develop a meaningful set of choices.

According to the *Handbook of Decision Analysis* [12], our goal should be to develop a set of alternatives that is *feasible, complete, compelling, and diverse.* By being feasible, we mean that the choice must not be impossible to pursue. In our early stage of brainstorming choices, it is okay to ignore financial and other constraints, but before we finalize our set of choices, we must eliminate the ones that are just downright infeasible. By being complete, we mean that we need to ensure that we have carefully defined what the choice includes and excludes. Full, clear definitions and descriptions are essential. By being compelling, we mean that each choice that we are seriously considering has something that strongly favors it and makes it appealing. There is no point in including "throw away choices" just for the sake of having more choices. By being diverse, we mean that the choices should have some significant differences from each other and not just vary by small increments. That said, it is a good practice to always include the "do nothing" alternative since that is almost always a viable choice. It is also a good practice to include a hypothetical "ideal" alternative which has all of the features that would lead to highest values on all value measures. By including an ideal alternative, when we conclude the evaluation, we can see where our best choice falls short of what we would really like.

How many choices should we include? The answer is an unsatisfactory "it depends." In the military, officers learn that they always should have at least three alternatives. Unfortunately, all too often, we've seen that rule applied poorly. That is particularly true in procuring new weapon systems. We'll often see one alternative that is so "gold-plated" that everyone wants it but is completely unaffordable, one alternative that is very inexpensive but has so little capability that no one wants it, and one alternative which is the one that the proponent really wants! In essence, there is no real choice built into the set of alternatives. For many decision makers and entrepreneurs, generating choices is relatively easy. A realtor can generate a long list of possibilities on paper and then use screening criteria to reduce the set to a manageable number that a client can visit. An insurance agent typically has a limited set of favored providers from which to choose. As a general rule, when we look at the set of choices as a whole, it should include enough choices to "touch" all of the objectives that we have defined. A well thought-out set of choices goes a long way in making better decisions. In the words of Shimon Peres, former Nobel Peace Prize-Winning President of Israel,

"When you have two alternatives, the first thing you have to do is to look for the third that you didn't think about, that doesn't exist."

In cases where the choices are not obvious, we may need to generate them ourselves, guided by our objectives. We find it useful to do this in two stages. First, there is a **divergent** stage in which we let the creative juices flow. We try to generate many diverse ideas without judging whether they are good or bad. Wild and crazy ideas are acceptable! We use our vision statement, issues list, and objectives hierarchy to spark innovative thought. Once we have a rich set of possibilities, we move into a **convergent** stage where we try to pare down the set of choices to a small number of well-designed alternatives for evaluation. The first stage involves a lot of individual or even group creativity, whereas the second stage benefits from highly organized, logical thinking.

THE STRATEGY TABLE

A useful tool in developing a series of choices is the strategy table. We can illustrate a strategy table in the context of a simple decision – what should we order at the Chinese restaurant? There are many choices for the complete meal and, for our purposes, we will define a meal as having a soup component, an appetizer component, an entrée component, a dessert component, and a beverage component. Let's say the chart below reflects the menu. The five components of the decision are shown as the columns and the choices within each component are shown within each column. Note that we don't read across the rows – we pick one selection from each column, and the rows themselves are meaningless. It's the old "pick one from column A, one from column B, etc." drill. We will have defined a meal when we have selected one choice from each column. The row in which the choice is located has no meaning since the entries are not related across rows.

Decision Components				
Soups	Appetizers	Entrees	Desserts	Beverage
None	None	Chicken lo mein	None	Water
Wonton	Fried wontons	Beef and broccoli	Fortune cookies	Iced tea
Eggdrop	Dumplings	Mongolian lamb	Fried ice cream	Soda
Hot and sour	Lettuce wraps	Steamed vegetables		Wine
	Lobster rolls	Peking duck		Champagne

Depending on our mood and the occasion, we might select different choices. If it is near the end of the month and the budget is tight, the "theme" for the meal may be "Low budget." If we have been trying to lose a few pounds, the theme may be "Low calorie." If it is just an ordinary night out, the theme may be "Regular dinner." Or if it is our anniversary and we feel like splurging, the theme may be "Special occasion." We can expand the strategy table to reflect our themes and to indicate what we would choose for each theme. For example, the "Low budget" theme can be represented by the circles in the strategy table below.

	Decision Components				
Strategies	Soups	Appetizers	Entrees	Desserts	Beverage
Low budget ●	None ●	None ●	Chicken lo mein ●	None	Water
Low calorie	Wonton	Fried wontons	Beef and broccoli	Fortune cookies ●	Iced tea
Regular dinner	Eggdrop	Dumplings	Mongolian lamb	Fried ice cream	Soda ●
Special occasion	Hot and sour	Lettuce wraps	Steamed vegetables		Wine
		Lobster rolls	Peking duck		Champagne

We can add the other themes to the table using different shapes to represent them. Notice that we can include the same choice in more than one theme. (Remember, in this layout, don't just read across the row associated with the theme but, instead, follow the associated shape.) For example, fortune cookies are included in both the Low calorie and Regular dinner alternatives in the chart below:

	Decision Components				
Strategies	Soups	Appetizers	Entrees	Desserts	Beverage
Low budget ●	None ●	None ●	Chicken lo mein ●	None ▲	Water ▲
Low calorie ▲	Wonton ●▲	Fried wontons	Beef and broccoli	Fortune ● cookies ●	Iced tea
Regular dinner ●	Eggdrop	Dumplings ●	Mongolian lamb ●	Fried ice cream ■	Soda ●
Special occasion ■	Hot and sour ■	Lettuce wraps ▲	Steamed ▲ vegetables		Wine ●
		Lobster rolls ■	Peking duck ■		Champagne ■

If you find it easier to represent a theme by reading straight across a row and not using shapes, that is acceptable. In that layout, the table would look like the table below and would be read in a conventional manner. The disadvantage of this approach is that the choices in the columns that weren't included in the displayed themes would no longer be visible (for example, the dumplings) and may be forgotten as possibilities if new themes are added:

	Decision Components				
Strategies	Soups	Appetizers	Entrees	Desserts	Beverage
Low budget	None	None	Chicken lo mein	Fortune cookies	Soda
Low calorie	Wonton	Lettuce wraps	Steamed vegetables	None	Water
Regular dinner	Wonton	Fried wontons	Mongolian lamb	Fortune cookies	Wine
Special occasion	Hot and sour	Lobster rolls	Peking duck	Fried ice cream	Champagne

The strategy table has enabled us to take what were originally hundreds of possible combinations and pare the choices down to a manageable set of four.

One of the better software tools for developing strategy tables is *DPL* which is described in Appendix C.

Let's take a look at another case study to illustrate the strategy table as a great tool for communicating the features of a decision.

CASE STUDY: INSURANCE PROFESSIONAL ALIZA LEITER – DEVELOPING THE STRATEGY TABLE

Aliza Leiter is an insurance professional who has been practicing for more than 30 years, specializing in disability insurance. She has seen the industry change greatly with the advent of the Internet. In the "good old days," clients would come to her for advice and, for the most part, would accept her recommendations with few questions. Today, clients, having searched the Internet, come far more prepared with both good and bad information. They want better explanations, and they want more of a say in customizing their coverages. Aliza recently attended a seminar on **FOCCUSSED** decision making, and thinks that the strategy table that she learned about would help her better communicate with her clients. She first lists the general features of disability policies and the choices that can be made for each feature:

1. Insurance continuation features

    a. no provision

    b. non-cancelable and guaranteed renewable

    c. guaranteed renewable

    d. conditionally renewable

    e. renewable at the insurance company's option

2. Amount of coverage

    a. 60% of pre-tax Income

    b. 50% of pre-tax income

    c. 40% of pre-tax income

3. Definition of disability

    a. own occupation

    b. any occupation in which you are working

    c. any occupation for which trained/experienced

    d. any occupation

    e. split definition

4. Elimination period

    a. None

    b. 30 days

    c. 60 days

    d. 90 days

e. 180 days

f. 360 days

5. Accumulation period

    a. none

    b. 180 days

    c. 360 days

6. Coverages

    a. accidents only

    b. accidents and sickness

7. Length of coverage

    a. short term

    b. long term

    c. lifetime

8. Residual and partial disability

    a. none

    b. partial

    c. residual

9. Cost of living increases

    a. none

    b. COLA adjustment, 3%

    c. COLA adjustment, 4%

    d. COLA adjustment, 5%

    e. COLA adjustment, 6%

10. Future Insurance options

a. none

b. up to age 55

c. up to age 65

11. Social Security integration

    a. non-integrated

    b. integrated

12. Other Options

    a. accidental death and dismemberment rider

    b. conversion to LTC

    c. exclusions

    d. presumptive disability

    e. return of premium

    f. recurrent disability

    g. waiver of premium

This is a lot for a client to absorb, and Aliza believes that organizing the information as a strategy table will help. The result is shown below. There is still a lot for her clients to absorb, but the choices they can make are easier to see:

Disability Insurance Decision Components							
Insurance continuation features	no provision	non-cancelable, guaranteed renewable	guaranteed renewable	conditionally renewable	renewable at company's option		
Amount of coverage (% pre-tax income)	60%	50%	40%				
Definition of disability	own occ	any occ, working	any occ, trained/experience	any occupation	split definition		
Elimination period (days)	0	30	60	90	180	360	
Accumulation period (days)	0	180	360				
Coverages	accidents only	accidents & sickness					
Length of coverage	short term	long term	lifetime				
Residual and partial disability	none	partial	residual				
Cost of living increases (COLA)	none	3%	4%	5%	6%		
Future insurance options	none	up to age 55	up to age 65				
Social Security integration	no	yes					
Other Options	AD&D	convert to LTC	exlusions	presumptive disability	return of premium	recurrent disability	waiver of premium

After doing this for many years, Aliza also knows that most of her clients will describe themselves when it comes to disability insurance in one of five ways:

Category 1 - I know I need disability coverage, but I can't afford much. I want a basic policy that will replace most of my income for a worst-case disability scenario. Keep it as cheap as you can.

Category 2 - I can't afford much, but I want more than the bare bones. Give me the features that make my premium dollars go the farthest, but forget the "bells and whistles."

Category 3 - I'd like a middle-of-the-road policy in terms of both protection and cost. Select the features that give me pretty good "bang-for-the-buck."

Category 4 - I want a good, solid disability policy that offers a lot of protection, but I don't want to go overboard; I'm willing to pay more in premiums for some of the "nice-to-haves," but I don't want the costs to go sky-high.

Category 5 - The thought of getting disabled scares the heck out of me. I can afford "gold-plated" coverage that gives me maximum protection with all of the "bells and whistles."

Knowing this, Aliza has prepared a set of recommendations for each of these categories as shown below in the matrix form of the strategy table. For each category, we can read across the chart to learn its specific features:

Disability Insurance Decision Components

Category	Insurance continuation features	Amount of coverage (% pre-tax income)	Definition of disability	Elimination period (days)	Accumulation period (days)	Coverages	Length of coverage	Residual and partial disability	Cost of living increases (COLA)	Future insurance options	Social Security integration	Other Options
Cat 1	guaranteed renewable	50%	any occupation	180	180	accidents	short term (5 yrs)	none	none	none	yes	none
Cat 2	non-cancelable, guaranteed renewable	50%	split definition	180	180	accidents	long term (age 65)	none	3%	none	yes	none
Cat 3	non-cancelable, guaranteed renewable	60%	any occ, trained/ experience	180	180	accidents & sickness	long term (age 65)	partial & residual	5%	none	yes	none
Cat 4	non-cancelable, guaranteed renewable	60%	own occ	90	360	accidents & sickness	lifetime	partial & residual	5%	up to 55	yes	waiver of premium, AD&D
Cat 5	non-cancelable, guaranteed renewable	60%	own occ	60	360	accidents & sickness	lifetime	partial & residual	6%	up to 65	no	waiver of premium, AD&D, LTC

For those of her clients who don't fit into any of the five categories, Aliza can use the strategy table to customize a policy.

Barriers to the Creative Process

The creative process of generating choices can be fun, but it is not always easy. There are many things that get in the way of creative thought. James Adams, in *Conceptual Blockbusting* [13], puts these blocks into four categories:

1. **Perceptual blocks** – these tend to relate to how we frame the problem and include things such as the tendency to over-constrain the problem (remember the tomato picker example?) or to under-constrain the problem, the inability to look at the problem from more than one perspective, and being biased by seeing what we expect or hope to see rather than what is actually there.

2. **Emotional blocks** – these focus on the psychological aspects of being creative in defining our choices such as fear of failure and risk taking, resistance to changing the status quo because it may cause chaos, and the tendency to be too quick to judge ideas rather than letting them mature.

3. **Cultural and environmental blocks** – these are the result of our surroundings that influence and mold the way we think. They include conforming to societal "no-no's" that prematurely limit what may be doable, taking decision making too seriously and not allowing room for humor and crazy thoughts, and perceiving a lack of support from those around us.

4. **Intellectual and expressive blocks** – these include the inability to approach a decision using more than one decision-making "language" or style (some people are great at the mathematics of decision making, some are more visually and graphically oriented), the inability to sort valid information

from invalid information, and the inability to communicate ideas to others.

CASE STUDY: MIKE AND MADDIE – DEVELOPING THE STRATEGY TABLE

Now, it is time to get back to Mike and Maddie and see how they are faring in coming up with some good franchising choices to evaluate based on their objectives. Mike has searched the Internet and is overwhelmed by the choices that are out there. He has also visited several facilities in his area posing as a potential member to learn first-hand as much as he could about the chains. He decides to use a strategy table to help get focused and to narrow down his choices. He has many things to consider in defining his alternatives:

Nature of the franchise: There are some promising opportunities to be the first in his general location or nearby locations for newer chains with no existing same-chain competition. He also has found a couple of existing facilities that are looking for a new franchisee.

Size of the franchise chain: Mike sees the number of units in the chain as a sign of stability, and he has found some offerings with franchises that have less than 10 locations, some with hundreds of locations, and still others with more than 1000 locations.

Size of the facility: Mike has found opportunities that run the gamut from relatively small fitness centers to facilities that are super-sized mega sports clubs with huge memberships.

Exercise offerings: Mike has identified some franchises that focus strictly on basic exercise and related training, some that offer many and diverse classes in addition to basic fitness training, and some opportunities with full scope sports clubs that offer everything from soup to nuts.

Non-exercise offerings: Mike sees non-exercise offerings such as juice bars or snack bars as welcome additions to revenues, but isn't sure if those features are worth the additional headaches. He is willing to consider opportunities with small juice bars or snack bars, but isn't ready to deal with things such as a full-scale restaurant on the premises. That would almost be like taking on both franchises he had considered instead of just one of them.

Net worth and liquid cash available start-up requirements: Mike has been surprised by the wide range of requirements from chain to chain. His net worth is in the vicinity of $100,000, and he has almost $50,000 in liquid cash available, but after talking informally to his neighbor and friend Jack, who is a loan officer for a local bank, he believes that he can get prequalified for loans that would allow him to think bigger.

Franchise commitment: Mike has been surprised to learn that some chains don't require the owner to be on the premises full time. His intent has been to run the club himself as a full-time job, but is pleased to see that there are opportunities that will permit far less of a commitment.

Number of employees needed: Not knowing the industry well, Mike is concerned about his ability to find and keep qualified employees. He has managed a dozen employees before, but has no experience with managing several dozen employees and that has him worried. He has discovered that the smaller facilities require very few full-time employees, but as he looks at some larger franchises, he realizes that "people management" may play a large part in his daily efforts.

Same chain competition: It seems as if Mike sees a McDonald's every few blocks from his house, and he is really worried about selecting a chain that has too many franchisees too close to each other within a small area. He notices that some of the advertised opportunities have no competition within a 25-mile distance of the advertised locations, while others, particularly the big chains such as L.A. Fitness, have clubs within 10 miles of each other.

Level of third-party support: Since this is a new venture for Mike, he really prefers to have as much support from his franchise chain as possible, particularly in the first few years. He has learned that some provide virtually no support other than initial training, while others provide extensive third-party support (for a fee) for the most important functions such as accounting, marketing, and maintenance.

State-of-the art-equipment: In his visits to fitness facilities, he has seen a huge difference in variety, condition, and state-of-the art in terms of the exercise equipment available at a location. It seems clear that, in general, the lower cost, lower membership-fee facilities offer far less than the more expensive facilities (more expensive to both the franchisee and to the members).

Length of the lease: This is a two-edged sword for Mike. He likes the stability that a long-term lease offers him but, since this is his first attempt and he is not sure how well it will go, having an "off-ramp" after a couple of years has its appeal. He has found some leases for as few as two or three years and others for as many as 10 years.

Membership incentives offered by the chain: Mike recognizes that the key to success is a robust and happy membership. This is a competitive business, and it often takes incentives, financial and otherwise, for a new member to enroll. He has seen that some chains offer virtually no incentives from the corporate level, while others are very aggressive in attracting new members.

Mike has organized his thoughts into the following strategy table that reflects the menu of major choices that he must make:

Components of the Decision					
Nature of franchise	Existing	New			
Size of the franchise chain	Less than ten locations	Hundreds of locations	More than 1000 locations		
Size of the facility	Small	Medium	Large	Mega	
Exercise offerings	Basic exercise facility	Basic + a few classes	Basic + many varied classes	Basic plus other sports	Full scope club
Non-exercise facilities	None	Juice bar	Snack bar	Restaurant	
Net worth & liquid cash available start-up requirements	Low	Medium	High	Very high	
Franchisee commitment	Absentee owner allowed	Physical presence required			
Number of employees needed	Low	Medium	High		
Same chain competition nearby	No	Yes			
Level of third-party support	Low	Medium	High	Full service	
State-of-the-art equipment	None	Some	All		
Length of lease (years)	2	3	5	10	
Membership incentives offered by chain	None	Limited	Aggressive		

After studying the strategy table, he has decided to develop four possible directions that he'd like to explore further before honing in on specific opportunities. He has decided to eliminate the high startup cost, full scope facilities, at least until he has some experience under his belt. He uses the matrix form of the strategy table to flesh out the features of these four choices and he has given them catchy names to reflect their focus:

1. **Crawl, walk, run** – In this choice, Mike would start slow with a smaller effort in a new franchise that he can mold to his preferences. This would require low investment that is well within his reach, but he would need a small amount of back-room support from the franchise chain.

2. **Steady as she goes** – In this choice, Mike would look for a small- to moderate-sized established franchise with a stable membership base. He'd prefer not to borrow any cash and would like the start-up requirements to be within range of his financial situation. He would need a moderate amount of back-room support from the franchise chain.

3. **Nothing ventured, nothing gained** – In this choice, Mike would go with an established facility in a chain that is well-established and relatively stable with hundreds of nationwide locations. Mike is willing to take on some non-exercise add-ons such as a juice bar, but doesn't want such activities to detract from his attention to his main focus, namely the exercise aspect of the business. He wants a franchise with quality, well-maintained equipment, some of which is state-of-the-art, to attract serious exercise buffs. He'll need a lot of third-party support for accounting, marketing, maintenance, and other back-room functions. For taking on this level of risk, he expects at least a five-year lease.

4. **Go for the gold** – In this choice, Mike would jump in with both feet and take an established or new franchise with one of the major national fitness players that has more than 1,000 locations nation-wide. He is willing to take on some non-exercise add-ons such as a juice bar or even a snack bar, but a restaurant is a step too far. He believes he can bring on an HR

person to deal with the kinds of employee issues that will inevitably arise when having dozens of employees. He will definitely have to borrow large sums of money to meet the initial financial requirements. He would be looking for full third-party support. For taking on this level of risk, he expects at least a 10-year lease.

Mike's choices can be summarized in the matrix form of the strategy table as shown on the next page:

Strategy	Components of the Decision												
	Nature of franchise	Size of the franchise chain	Size of the facility	Exercise offerings	Non-exercise facilities	Net worth & liquid cash available start-up requirements	Franchise commitment	Number of employees needed	Same chain competition nearby	Level of third-party support	State-of-the-art equipment	Length of lease (years)	Membership incentives offered by chain
1. Crawl, walk, run	New	Less than ten locations	Small	Basic exercise facility	None	Low	Physical presence required	Low	No	Low	None	2	Limited
2. Steady as she goes	Existing	Dozens of locations	Small to Medium	Basic + a few classes	None	Medium	Absentee owner allowed	Medium	No	Medium	None	3	Limited
3. Nothing ventured, nothing gained	Existing locations	Hundreds of locations	Large	Basic + many varied classes	Juice bar	Medium to high	Absentee owner allowed	Medium to high	Yes	High	Some	5	Aggressive
4. Go for the gold	Existing or new	More than 1000 locations	Mega	Basic plus other sports	Juice/snack bar	Very high	Physical presence required	Full service	Yes	Full service	All	10	Aggressive

Mike feels pretty confident that he understands his range of choices. He can't wait to evaluate them against his objectives so he can decide on the general direction that he wants to pursue. Once he decides on that, it will be an easy task to select and evaluate specific opportunities. Maddie shares his enthusiasm and, for the first time since they began their investigation, their fears and angst are turning to excitement.

Post-script from Omar on Choices – Omar and Indie

The title of this section isn't a reference to the latest Steven Spielberg action/adventure film. It's a reference to a decision-making process I went through in deciding how to publish my books. The question I faced was one faced by all authors: faced with limited options, should I seek traditional publishing or self-publish (called "Indie" these days).

The answer seems obvious at first. Traditional publishing would seem the obvious way to go and that, at first, was my inclination. Unfortunately, the traditional option didn't pay out for my first book so I chose the only option available and I published it myself. "Chose" is an interesting choice of words, don't you think, because that really was my only option at the time. As they say in the trade, I "started the fire" by selling more than 50,000 copies of my book on my own. That success got the attention of the publishing world and I was offered a traditional contract. Success at last, right?

Well, as usual, that depends on your definition of success. I quickly discovered that the traditional publishing route for a new author wasn't all I thought it was cracked up to be. First, there's the matter of money. The rule of thumb in publishing states that authors earn 8 to 12 percent of the cover price of their book. If your name is Stephen

King or J.K. Rowling you can negotiate a better deal I'm sure, but for a first-timer I was looking at earning at the lowest end of the spectrum. Think about that. After all the labor of writing a book, somebody else earns up to 90 percent or more off my labor. As a friend once said, "Why is that a good idea?"

Additionally, regardless of what they say, traditional publishers will make only minimal promotional efforts for a first-time author. That's obvious. It's business. If you're a traditional publishing house where are you going to put your promotional dollars – with Stephen King or Omar Periu?

The more I looked into Indie publishing, the more I liked that option. Sure, I had to do most of the promotion and public relations myself, but that's really no more effort than I'd have to make through the traditional route. The big difference I discovered was in the revenue stream. For example, I researched one of the major book distributors, Amazon, and made an interesting discovery. Depending upon how the author prices his or her book, the author earns between 35 and 70 percent of the cover price. (I chose the 70 percent option.)

What's the lesson learned? Let's just say that I've published fifteen books since 1999. Thirteen of them are Indie published works.

RAPID RECAP: CREATING CHOICES

- **Choices** are the elements of a decision over which we have control. We get to define the set of choices that we want to evaluate in a way that best meets our objectives.

- **Satisficing** is a decision-making strategy that entails searching through the available choices until we find one that "clears our threshold."

- In the **FOCCUSSED** approach to decision making, we attempt to find the *best* alternative available. For most of us, "good enough" isn't acceptable and we prefer to make the optimal decision.

- Our goal should be to develop alternatives that are **feasible, complete, compelling, and diverse.**

- When we look at the set of choices as a whole, it should include enough choices to "touch" all of the objectives that we have defined.

- In generating creative choices, we first go through a **divergent** "wild and crazy" stage followed by a highly organized **convergent** stage.

- The **strategy table** is a useful tool for generating creative and diverse choices and for communicating with others.

- We need to be aware of the blocks that can impede creativity in order to overcome them.

"Destiny is not a matter of chance; it is a matter of choice.
It is not a thing to be waited for, it is a thing to be achieved."

~William Jennings Bryant

Chapter 5: Identifying Consequences

"We are free to choose our paths, but we can't choose the consequences that come with them."

~Sean Covey, *The 7 Habits of Highly Effective Teens*

We are well on our way to being **FOCCUSSED** decision makers in that we know how to properly frame a problem, identify our objectives, and generate creative choices. The next step is to understand the Consequences of making a choice in terms of how we value the events that may unfold.

Identifying Consequences and Measuring Values

We first need to make sure that we understand the decision-making terminology that we are using. Let's use a simple example to define our terms. I'm going to flip a coin. If you call it correctly, you win $10, but if you call it incorrectly, you win nothing. We know that there is uncertainty in whether the flip will be "heads" or "tails" (we will deal with uncertainty in the next chapter). We refer to the **outcomes** of an event as the possibilities that may occur: for the coin flip, the outcomes are "heads" or "tails" or "land on its side" (which we will ignore!). We refer to a **consequence** as what will happen if an outcome occurs. The consequence of calling the coin correctly is "win $10," and the consequence of calling it incorrectly is "win $0." But there is still another aspect that we must consider – what is the **value** of the consequence to us. In our coin flip example, winning $10 may mean different things to different people. To the college student living on ramen noodles, $10 may have great value. To Donald Trump (we know he's rich, he has told us so), $10 is almost meaningless. Clearly, value is a personal issue and is highly **dependent upon context. Recall that one of the three pillars of FOCCUSSED** decision making was preferences (alternatives and information were the others), and we use values to express these preferences.

We'll give you fair warning. We need to get a little technical on this topic, but nothing too deep. We'll show you some easy approaches towards evaluating consequences as well as some more sophisticated ones. The nice thing is that you can pick the techniques that fit your comfort level and not worry about the rest.

We can measure values in a variety of ways, but the two most common are to use a **relative approach** in which we directly compare things to each other and an **absolute approach** in which we define a specific measurement scale that can be used to get a consistent measure from one consequence to another. For example, we can use a relative approach to visually order from tallest to shortest 10 people in a room, or we can use an absolute approach with a tape measure to get an exact measure for height in inches. The relative approach is quicker but less accurate, and the absolute approach takes longer but is far more accurate.

Hot Tip: *Most people are terrible at making absolute numerical judgments and are better at making relative judgments. Rather than eliciting numbers, it is usually better to elicit relationships and to infer the numbers from them.*

Recall that in making decisions, we need to evaluate our choices in terms of our objectives, and that is where values come into play. We will need some sort of scale, either relative or absolute, to compare the choices on each objective. Let's start with the easier approach, relative measurement.

CASE STUDY: WENDI LEE – COMPARING CHOICES

In an earlier chapter, Wendi Lee identified objectives and measures for her mobile computing decision. We'll use four of her lower-level objectives to illustrate how to compare choices as follows:

- Minimize weight to include peripherals and cords

- Maximize battery life

- Provide a minimum of 128 gigabytes of internal storage with capability for adding external storage devices

- Minimize acquisition cost (without added software)

Wendi used a strategy table to identify possible choices, and narrowed them down to three configurations:

1. MacBook Air Hi resolution laptop (11 inch screen version)

2. Dell portable Latitude 7000 (12 inch screen version)

3. Microsoft Surface Pro 3 Tablet (12 inch screen version)

She has done her homework and has developed a consequences table that shows the characteristics of her choices on each of the objectives:

Consequence Table	Choices		
Characteristics	Macbook Air	Dell Latitude 7000	Microsoft Surface Pro 3
Carrying weight (lbs.)	2.38	2.76	1.76
Battery life (hrs.)	9	7	8
Internal storage (Gigabytes)	526	128	256
Acquisition cost ($)	1099	1175	999

For simplicity, let's assume, for the time being, that these four characteristics are all that Wendi cares about. Without doing any further analysis, it is easy to see that the MacBook Air is better than the Dell Latitude on all of the characteristics. It is not usually the case that one choice is better than another on everything, but when it does happen, we can say that the better choice dominates the other choice. In our example, the Dell is dominated by the MacBook. Not only that, the Dell is dominated by the Surface Pro 3 as well since the Dell is worse on all four characteristics. In comparing the MacBook with the Surface, we see that the MacBook is better on battery life and storage, but the Surface is better on carrying weight and cost.

We can take an easy approach and convert the consequences table into a ranking table by replacing the performance characteristic with the rank. For example, on battery life, the MacBook ranks first, the Surface Pro 3 ranks second, and the Dell ranks third. A complete ranking table would look like the following:

Ranking Table	Choices		
Characteristics	MacBook Air	Dell Latitude 7000	Microsoft Surface Pro 3
Carrying weight (lbs.)	2	3	1
Battery life (hrs.)	1	3	2
Internal storage (Gigabytes)	1	3	2
Acquisition cost ($)	2	3	1

The obvious question is "which choice is best across all four characteristics?" It would be tempting to add the ranks for a choice down a column, and then select the choice with the lowest total since a lower number means a better rank. We see this done all of the time but, unfortunately, it can be a fatal mistake. Ranks are fine for ordering things but, unless you turn to some pretty sophisticated rank-oriented formulas (beyond the scope of this book), you can't do simple math on ranks. The math is basically meaningless, and the reason for that is we have no sense of how far apart rankings are. Choices that rank 1 and 2 on a characteristic may be very close together or very far apart in how they are valued, and the rank just doesn't convey that information. So don't fall into the trap of using ranks to combine things. There are more appropriate ways to do that, and we'll be covering some techniques that address both of the issues raised above. While the ranking approach does give us insight into how our choices compare on a relative basis, it doesn't help us much in answering "which is best?"

DEVELOPING SCORING SCALES

Can we do better than ranking? The answer is yes, by moving to an approach called scaling. Simply put, we define scales that can be used for direct measurements. We saw an example of that in the example of measuring height in inches earlier in this chapter. Some things, such as height, cost, storage, and fuel economy have **natural measures** (inches, dollars, gigabytes, and miles per gallon) and can be measured directly. Whenever we can, we try to use **natural scales**. However, some things don't have natural measures such as the quality of a dive in Olympic diving competitions. In these cases, we develop what are known as **constructed scales**. The Olympic judges have a well-defined scale that runs from 1 to 10 with clear (but subjective) definitions of what a diver must do to get a particular number on the scale. But unlike the rankings that we talked about, the 1 to 10 scale is developed in a way that enables us to do some math on the numbers. Whether we use natural scales or constructed scales, we want the scales to allow us to calculate ratios of numbers. This just means that if one choice is valued at 10 on the scale, and another at 5, the first is twice as valuable as the second (that is where the term ratio comes in to play). 28 miles per gallon is twice as much as 14 miles per gallon, so miles per gallon is another example of a ratio-based scale. The key quality required for ratios is that the scale has to have a true zero – a total absence of the characteristic really must mean zero. Here is an example of what can get us into trouble. Is a $90°$ Fahrenheit day twice as hot as a $45°$ day? At first glance, it would appear so since the ratio of 90 to 45 is two to one. But what if we were in Europe and the temperature was expressed in Centigrade? $90°$ converts to $32°$ and $45°$ converts to $7°$. Clearly, we no longer have a two to one ratio! Without going into detail, as long as our scales reflect good ratios, we will be able to deal with this issue.

We can also construct what we call word, or adjectival scales for measurement. A measure can run from very low, to low, to moderate, to high, to very high, and we can assign numbers to these words that can be used for calculations. As long as the numbers maintain the ratio property, we are just fine. Instead of words, we can use symbols such as stars as used in the *J.D. Power* auto ratings or *Trip Advisor* hotel ratings. It helps to distinguish between how a choice performs (the consequence) which we call a **"score,"** and the number that reflects our preference for that level of performance which we call a **"value."**

We'll now look at examples of scales that we find very useful for comparing choices. We can use a **Word Scale** or a **Star Scale** to compare choices characteristic by characteristic. For every word score or star score, assume that there is a good definition of what it takes to get that score. Unfortunately, that doesn't give us any way to combine across characteristics using sound math.

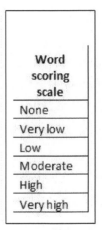
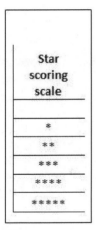

We can solve that problem by associating a ratio value scale with either of these types of scoring scales. We can use 0 to 1, 0 to 10, 0 to 100, or any other endpoints that we choose. We prefer 0 to 100 scales because we don't have to deal with decimals and the scale is wide enough to discriminate among the choices. For the word scoring scale, it might look like the scale shown below. For those who are more visual, a graph of what this might look like is also shown below. The horizontal axis of the graph represents the score, and the vertical axis represents the value. For those who don't like numbers, we've color-coded the scale in shades of gray and black – the darker the color, the better.

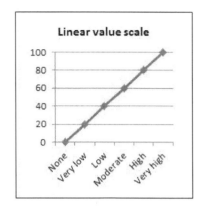

Word scoring scale	Linear value scale
None	0
Very low	20
Low	40
Moderate	60
High	80
Very high	100

We can take an easy approach for the value scale and assume that it follows a straight line (called a linear scale) as shown above with every increase in scoring level getting the same number of additional value points. Alternatively, we can assume that different increases in scoring levels get us different increases in value points (a nonlinear scale) as shown below:

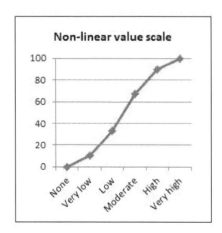

Word scoring scale	Nonlinear value scale
None	0
Very low	10
Low	33
Moderate	67
High	90
Very high	100

The curves can take on many different shapes depending on what the value scale is intending to convey.

Let's say we are comparing cars' fuel economy using miles per gallon (MPG) as the performance measure and we use the linear scale. Since MPG is a natural measure, we can use the first column for the score. A car that gets 45 MPG would get a value of 80, whereas a car with a score of 24 MPG would get a value of 40. Now, let's compare the cars on comfort which has no natural measure. We can use the word scale or the star scale. A car with a "very high" score on comfort would get a value of 100, while one with "moderate" comfort would get a value of 67. As mentioned earlier, when we associate a value of zero with a score, we really mean that we perceive no value for that level of performance. Notice that there is no requirement that the scoring scales for the different characteristics be the same for each, as long as we can relate a value with a score for each scale:

Natural scoring scale (miles per gallon)	Linear value scale		Comfort scoring scale	Non-linear value scale
5	0		None	0
12	20		Very low	10
24	40		Low	33
37	60		Moderate	67
45	80		High	90
58	100		Very high	100

There is one very important thing to note. When we were using rankings, we had to know what our choices were up front before we could develop the ranking. When we were developing the absolute scales, we did not need to know the choices, which is totally in keeping with value-focused thinking. The scales were *based on our objectives and what performance characteristics we valued*, not on the specific performance of a pre-determined set of choices. That is a very powerful difference.

> **Hot Tip:** *When analyzing a decision, don't fall in love with the numbers. They are primarily a means of exchanging information and having a discussion about the decision opportunity. The audit trail of rationale behind the numbers is often more important.*

CASE STUDY: WENDI LEE – DEVELOPING VALUE SCALES

Now, we can go back to Wendi's computing decision and improve on her rankings by using better scales. Wendi developed value scales (not shown) and used them to complete the table below. The values are consistent with her rankings, but provide a greater level of discrimination among the choices. If we assume, for now, that each characteristic carries equal impact on the decision, we can add the values down each column to get a total value for each choice. With the information provided, the Microsoft Surface Pro 3 would be a clear winner.

Value Table	Choices		
Characteristics	MacBook Air	Dell Latitude 7000	Microsoft Surface Pro 3
Carrying weight (lbs.)	40	30	100
Battery life (hrs.)	90	60	75
Internal storage (Gigabytes)	100	20	80
Acquisition cost ($)	70	40	95
Total value across characteristics	300	150	350
			⬆
			Best

In reality, for most decisions, the objectives will not have the same impact, and we will have to find a way to put more emphasis on one over another before we just add up the numbers. But that is for a later chapter.

CASE STUDY: MIKE AND MADDIE – DEVELOPING VALUE SCALES

And now, let's get back to Mike and Maddie and see how they are doing in evaluating their choices. When we last left them, they had identified their objectives and their value measures, and they had developed four choices to explore in more depth. Recall that Mike had three fundamental objectives, each broken down further:

1. Maximize long-term wealth from franchise ownership

   - Maximize the track record of success

   - Maximize opportunities for membership growth

     o Minimize competition

     o Maximize the ability to offer affordable memberships

     o Maximize the quality of the equipment

2. Maximize the enjoyment of the franchisee experience

   - Provide a franchise that will be enjoyable to own and operate

     o Maximize third-party support provided

   - Maximize the opportunity to attract and retain qualified staff

   - Maximize time available to spend with family without sacrificing franchise performance

   - Maximize flexibility in managing the franchise

- Minimize daily commuting time

3. Provide an economically viable business opportunity

- Minimize difference between owner's net worth/liquid cash available and franchise required net worth/liquid cash available

- Optimize investment costs

  o Minimize initial capital contribution/franchise fee

  o Minimize annual royalty fees

  o Minimize annual operating costs

  o Minimize annual equipment replacement costs.

- Maximize long-term job stability

  o Maximize the length of franchising agreement

Previously, Mike had identified how he would measure each objective and sub-objective by designating a value measure; now he must develop scoring and value scales that can be used to evaluate alternatives. If an objective is broken down into sub-objectives, the value measure is defined at the lowest level of the breakdown. For example, for the sub-objective "optimize investment costs," we can see that it is broken down into four lower-level objectives. It is at the lowest level that we develop the scoring and value scales. For "maximize long-term job stability," there is only one lower-level sub-objective, namely "maximize the length of the franchising agreement," and it is here that Mike must develop the scoring and value scales. For "maximize the track record of success," there is no further breakdown and so it is at this level that Mike must develop the scoring and value scale.

After several hours of effort, Mike has developed the scoring and value scales as shown in the three tables below. He decided to use a 0 to 100 ratio value scale for each value measure. He remembered Pareto's Rule and eliminated a few of the value measures as being less important. Mike really liked that he was able to develop the scales without knowing the specific choices that he will be evaluating – one of the big advantages of value-focused thinking. For the purposes of clarity in the tables, Mike used short titles for his sub-objectives and value measures.

1. Maximize long-term wealth from franchise ownership

Track record				Competition				Membership growth					
								Affordability		Equipment quality			
Average same-chain annual return on investment		Franchise 500 ranking		Miles to nearest same-chain competition		# of competing fitness franchises in zip code		Level of corporate incentives		Amount of state-of-the-art equipment		Variety and quantity of equipment	
Score	Value	Score	Value	Score	Value	Score	Value	Score	Value	Score	Value	Score	Value
< 20%	0	Bottom 50%	0	<3	0	>10	0	None	0	None	0	Low	0
20-29.9%	20	51-75%	30	3-5	33	6-10	20	Very low	10	A few pieces	40	Medium	60
30-39.9%	40	76-90%	60	6-10	67	3-5	50	Low	35	More than half	75	High	80
40-49.9%	60	91-98%	90	>10	100	1-2	90	Medium	65	Almost all	95	Very High	100
50-75%	80	99-100%	100			None	100	High	90	All	100		
>75%	100							Very high	100				

2. Maximize the enjoyment of the franchisee experience

Enjoyable ownership								Time with family			
Third-party support				Ability to attract and retain qualified staff				Management flexibility		Daily commute time	
Breadth of services provided		Quality of services provided		Average same-chain annual turnover rate		Competitive compensation package		Average hours per day spent at facility by same-chain franchisees		Availability of affordable housing within 20 minutes of facility	
Score	Value	Score	Value	Score	Value	Score	Value	Score	Value	Score	Value
Minimum support	0	Very low	0	>50%	0	Way under market	0	>16	0	Very low	0
Basic accounting	20	Low	30	26-50%	33	Below market	30	12-16	10	Low	35
Acctng & marketing	80	Medium	60	10-25%	67	Average market	60	10-11	35	Medium	65
All major 3rd-party	100	High	90	<10%	100	Above market	85	8-9	65	High	85
		Very high	100			Highly above market	100	4-7	90	Very high	100
								<4	100		

3. Provide an economically viable business opportunity									
Net worth and liquid cash available requirements				Investment costs				Long-term job stability	
Requirements vs. Mike's financial situation		Likelihood of obtaining required financing		Initial capital contribution		Annual royalty fee percentage		Length of lease (years)	
Score	Value	Score	Value	Score	Value	Score	Value	Score	Value
Too big a stretch	0	Very low	0	>$750K	0	7%	0	2	0
Borderline qualify	20	Low	30	$400-750K	50	6%	40	3	40
Doable, but will require financing	80	Medium	60	$100-399.9K	80	5%	75	5	75
Within Mike's financial resources	100	High	90	<$100K	100	4%	90	10	100
		Very high	100			3%	100		

Mike is almost ready to evaluate his choices. Recall from Chapter 4 that Mike had identified four high-level strategies as shown below. He and Maddie had since decided that "Go for the gold" was a bridge too far for them, but that they would consider specific opportunities from any of the other three strategies. Maddie is a bit more conservative and is leaning towards "Crawl, walk, run" since it starts relatively small; Mike is leaning towards "Nothing ventured, nothing gained."

Strategy	Nature of franchise	Size of the franchise chain	Size of the facility	Exercise offerings	Non-exercise facilities	Net worth & liquid cash available start-up requirements	Number of employees needed	Same chain competition nearby	Level of third-party support	State-of-the-art equipment	Length of lease (years)	Membership incentives offered by chain
1. Crawl, walk, run	New	Less than ten locations	Small	Basic exercise facility	None	Low	Low	No	Low	None	2	Limited
2. Steady as she goes	Existing	Dozens of locations	Small to Medium	Basic + a few classes	None	Medium	Medium	No	Medium	None	3	Limited
3. Nothing ventured, nothing gained	Existing	Hundreds of locations	Large	Basic + many varied classes	Juice bar	Medium to high	Medium to high	Yes	High	Some	5	Aggressive
4. Go for the gold	Existing or new	More than 1000 locations	Mega	Basic plus other sports	Juice/snack bar	Very high	Full service	Yes	Full service	All	10	Aggressive

Components of the Decision

By now, Mike was getting really psyched about making a decision, and he was ready to find specific franchising choices that seem to meet his objectives. Over the next few days, he hit the Internet hard and identified several alternatives that he wanted to evaluate using his value measures. The four franchises that he wanted to evaluate are summarized below:

For Your Health – This is a relatively new franchise with six locations in the N.Y.-N.J. area. It is looking for its first Florida location. There are seven competing fitness franchises in the same zip code. It requires the franchisee to be full time (40 hours a week). It has identified a facility within 15 minutes of Mike's house, and is in the process of purchasing and setting up equipment. All of the equipment will be new, but relatively low end. Staff turnover rate for the chain averages 12%/year. The facility is relatively small which will limit the amount of equipment that can be installed. In order to attract a loyal franchisee, it offers a five-year lease. Initial capital required is $75K and the franchisee must have a minimum net worth of $100K. Mike and Maddie believe that they can do this without outside financing. Annual royalties are 4%. The few franchises they have averaged a 52% Return on Investment, but the franchise is too new to be ranked by Franchise 500. The company offers very little third-party support other than initial training, but offers an average compensation package. There will be no food or drink sales other than vending machines. Because the chain is hungry for new clients, it offers aggressive incentives for the first year of membership. Maddie really likes this opportunity because it is consistent with a "crawl, walk, run" strategy.

Fit to Be Tied – This is a small chain with 15 locations in Florida, three of which are within 25 miles of Mike's current home, the nearest within six miles. There are eight competing fitness franchises in the same zip code. It prefers franchisees to be full-time (40 hours a week), but allows for part-timers and work-at-home franchisees. It is looking for a person to take over an existing franchise in Boca Raton since the existing franchisee has become very ill and can't continue. All of the equipment is less than three years old, with a few new, high-end multi-purpose machines. The emphasis is on individual training, but there are two or three group classes offered each day. There are several personal trainers affiliated with the facility, but they are not staff. There are six full-time employees who appear to be happy and doing a great job since only one employee has left in three years, and Customer Retention has been over 90%. It is rated at 60% in Franchise 500. The new franchisee can take over the existing lease which has two years remaining on it, or can request a new four-year lease. Initial capital required is $110K, and annual royalties are 5%. The franchisee must have a minimum net worth of $125K. This particular franchise has averaged a 65% Return on Investment which is a bit higher than the other franchises in the chain. The compensation package is also above market. The franchise offers initial training and marketing support, but offers none of the back room functions such as accounting. Few corporate incentives are offered to members. The previous franchisee had just signed a contract for a juice bar to be added to the facility. Mike believes that this opportunity would be consistent with his "steady as she goes" strategy.

Better Bodies Gym – This is a nationwide chain with more than 600 locations. It is rated in the top tier (92%) by Franchise 500. They are looking for a new franchisee in West Palm Beach, so Mike and Maddie would probably need to move to the area to make the opportunity more viable. That is a very upscale county, and it will be a bit harder for Mike and Maddie to find affordable housing. The nearest same-chain franchise is more than 100 miles away in Orlando, but there are six other fitness companies in the same or adjoining zip codes. Mike visited the Orlando facility and was excited to find a large facility with state-of-the-art equipment, plenty of it, and a ton of activity everywhere in the room. Staff turnover rate is a moderate 15%. At the proposed facility, there would be a juice bar and a snack bar, but they would be run by a separate franchisee with Mike being able to collect rent and a small percentage of sales. The chain has averaged a very healthy 77% annual Return on Investment for its Florida locations, and Mike has learned that there are several other candidates who have already expressed interest. Few incentives are offered to members. In order to retain franchisees, the chain offers a 10-year lease. The initial capital cost is high, $250K, so Mike would have to arrange for financing but, for qualified individuals, the chain itself will provide financing. Net worth and liquid cash available requirements are surprisingly low, but the royalty rate is 6%. Mike would have to be a full-time manager at the facility which, based on other locations, would require a staff of 25. The franchise offers full third-party support for training (included in the package), marketing, accounting, maintenance, and a few other things on a fee for service. The compensation package is considerably above market. Mike is really pumped up by the opportunity since it is consistent with his "nothing ventured, nothing gained" strategy.

Fitness Focus – This is a regional chain on the East Coast with 102 locations. It is highly rated in Franchise 500, being ranked in the top quarter (85%) of franchises. There is an existing franchise in Ft. Lauderdale that needs a new franchisee, and the closest same-chain facility is 25 miles away from it. There are only three competing fitness chains in the area, possibly because it is in an industrial part of the city. It is well equipped with many machines, most of which are state-of-the art. Staff turnover has been high, and ratings found on the Internet are very mixed. The chain provides training, marketing, and accounting third-party services. The compensation package is above average for the fitness market. Mike can be a part-time manager if he chooses, the current staff size is 15, but there doesn't appear to be a good candidate for a day-to-day on site manager among them. The initial capital required is $190K, and Mike thinks he could get financing. Annual royalty fees are 5%, but the length of the lease is an above average six years.

After studying all of the above information plus a lot more information that they found either online or through visits, Mike and Maddie have developed the consequence table below for the choices. They then used the previous value measure tables to convert the characteristics to a numerical score as shown in the value table (second table) below. In some cases, the scores for the alternatives fall between the points on the scoring scale, so Mike had to do his best to select a value closest to the defined scale points.

If Mike assumes that all value measures should be considered equally in the decision (a very bad assumption that will be corrected later), he can add up the values for each choice across all of the value measures to get the totals in the rightmost column of the second table. Mike sees that, at first glance, the highest valued choice is **Fitness Focus** with 1358 points. **Better Bodies Gym** and **Fit to Be Tied** did well also at 1257 points and 1247 points, respectively. **For Your Health** is clearly bringing up the rear with 1012 points.

Mike showed the results to Maddie, and both felt pretty comfortable with the top two choices, but something was nagging at Mike. When he did his scoring, there was a lot of uncertainty about how the alternatives would perform on several of the value measures, yet he hadn't been able to capture that uncertainty in a satisfying way. He wondered, would the results change if he were better able to reduce some of that uncertainty. And of course, as we'll see in the next chapter, the answer is definitely "yes."

Value measures	For Your Health	Fit To Be Tied	Better Bodies Gym	Fitness Focus
Average same-chain annual return on investment	52%	65%	77%	48%
Franchise 500 ranking	None	60%	92%	85%
Miles to nearest same-chain competition	No same chain close by	6	100	25
# of competing fitness franchises in zip code	7	8	6	3
Level of corporate incentives	Very high	Low	Low	High
Amount of state-of-the-art equipment	None	A few pieces	All	>50%
Variety and quantity of equipment	Low	High	Very high	High
Breadth of services provided	Training only	Training & marketing	All major 3rd-party	Training, accounting, marketing
Quality of services provided	Don't know	High	Very high	Medium
Average same-chain annual staff turnover rate	12%	<10%	15%	27%
Competitive compensation package	Average market	Above market	Highly above market	Above market
Average hours per day spent at facility by same-chain franchisees	10	6-8	12	6-8
Availability of affordable housing within 20 minutes	High	High	Low	High
Requirements vs. Mike's financial situation	Within financial resources	Doable, but will require financing	Borderline quality	Doable, but will require financing
Likelihood of obtaining required financing	None needed	High	Medium	High
Initial capital contribution	$75K	$110K	$250K	$190K
Annual royalty fee percentage	4%	5%	6%	5%
Length of lease (years)	5	4	10	6

Mike & Maddie's Value Table

Value measures	Choices	For Your Health	Fit To Be Tied	Better Bodies Gym	Fitness Focus
Average same-chain annual return on investment	Value	80	80	100	60
Franchise 500 ranking	Value	0	30	90	60
Miles to nearest same-chain competition	Value	100	67	100	100
# of competing fitness franchises in zip code	Value	20	20	20	50
Level of corporate incentives	Value	100	35	35	90
Amount of state-of-the-art equipment	Value	0	40	100	75
Variety and quantity of equipment	Value	0	80	100	80
Breadth of services provided	Value	0	60	100	85
Quality of services provided	Value	0	90	100	60
Average same-chain annual staff turnover rate	Value	67	100	67	33
Competitive compensation package	Value	60	85	100	85
Average hours per day spent at facility by same-chain franchisees	Value	35	90	10	90
Availability of affordable housing within 20 minutes	Value	85	85	35	85
Requirements vs. Mike's financial situation	Value	100	80	20	80
Likelihood of obtaining required financing	Value	100	90	60	90
Initial capital contribution	Value	100	80	80	80
Annual royalty fee percentage	Value	90	75	40	75
Length of lease (years)	Value	75	60	100	80
Total Value		1012	1247	1257	1358

The examples in this chapter were done in Excel, but some of our favorite software tools for building value hierarchies and value curves include *HIVIEW* and *Logical Decisions*, both described in Appendix C.

RAPID RECAP: IDENTIFYING CONSEQUENCES

- We refer to the **outcomes** of an event as the possibilities that may occur. We refer to a **consequence** as what will happen if an outcome occurs. We refer to values as a measure of how much we like or dislike a consequence.

- We can measure with a **relative approach** in which we directly compare things to each other or an **absolute approach** in which we define a specific measurement scale that can be used to get a consistent measure from one consequence to another. The relative approach is quicker but less accurate. The absolute approach takes longer but is far more accurate.

- Some things, such as height, cost, storage, and fuel economy have **natural measures** (inches, dollars, gigabytes, and miles per gallon) and can be measured directly. However, some things don't have natural measures such as the quality of a dive in Olympic diving competitions. In these cases, we develop what are known as **constructed scales**.

- We distinguish between how a choice performs (the consequence) which we call a **"score,"** and the number that reflects our preference for that level of performance which we call a **"value."**

- A **consequence table** is a useful tool for understanding how we can measure the consequences of our decisions. We can extend the consequence table into a value table by associating a numerical scale (usually 0 to 100) with each possible characteristic of a consequence.

- A **value table** converts the performance score on a value measure to a value that can be used to compare choices.

"When you choose an action, you choose the consequences of that action. When you desire a consequence you had damned well better take the action that would create it."

~Lois McMaster Bujold, *Memory*

NOTES:

Chapter 6: Incorporating Uncertainty

"The 50-50-90 rule: anytime you have a 50-50 chance of getting something right, there's a 90% probability you'll get it wrong."

~Andy Rooney , *60 Minutes TV Commentator*

"10% ago I was 90% unsure of what I didn't want to do.
Now I'm just 33.3% sure that I'm 66.6% unsure.
And I can say this with 0.1% certainty."

~Jarod Kintz, *Seriously Delirious, But Not At All Serious*

The quotes above are humorous, but the reality is that we are terrible at dealing with Uncertainty. Most people, when they have to talk in terms of probabilities, just don't get it. And there is a reason for that – dealing with probabilities is very difficult, even for those of us who deal with them every day in our work. Many of you last encountered probability theory in high school or college and, as soon as the courses were over, you hit the "memory dump" buttons in your brains. But if we are going to talk about sound decision making, we have to talk, at least in a broad sense, about dealing with uncertainty. Think of this probability review as the kind of vaccination that you had to get as a child – you knew it was going to hurt a bit, but it was necessary to avoid greater pain down the road!

If you were to implement the concepts of **FOCCUSSED** decision making that you've read about up to here and ignore this chapter on uncertainty, you would still be better decision makers. This chapter is more advanced and is somewhat challenging, but we are *not* going to try to make you experts in probability theory; we *are* going to try to give you a better sense of how to think about uncertain situations and to give you some simple techniques for incorporating probability into your thinking and decision making. Even if you only read the section on how to think about probabilities and bypass the more difficult case studies, you will get something valuable from the reading. And for those who are masochists and want to dig deeper into the subject of probability theory, there are some great references at the end of this book.

How Good Are You
at Thinking about Probability?

Let's see how well you think in probabilistic terms. We're going to pose four simple (hah!) questions whose answers are based on probabilistic thought, and we'll see how you do. If you get them all correct, you don't need to read the rest of this chapter - you are a whiz at dealing with uncertainty. We'll give you the answers at the end of the four questions.

1. You are in a room that has 50 people in it (counting yourself). What is the probability that there are two people in the room that have the same birthday (day and month, not year)?

2. In front of you are three chests, each with an upper and lower drawer. One chest has a gold coin in each drawer, one has a silver coin in each drawer, and one has one gold and one silver coin in the drawers (but you don't know if the gold is in the upper or lower drawer). You select a chest at random, pick one drawer, and see a gold coin. What is the probability that if you open the second drawer in the same chest, you will see another gold coin?

3. You are visiting Las Vegas and are playing the roulette wheel. A red number has come up seven times in a row. If you were betting on the next spin, would you bet on red or black?

4. You are a winning contestant on "Let's Make a Deal." You are playing for a new car. There are five keys on a rack and, if you select the key that starts the car, you win it. You've decided to pick key #1. The game show host tells you that he is going to make things easier for you to win, and he tells you that the winning key is not key #2 (he always tells the truth, and he knows which one is the winning key). He then offers you the opportunity to swap the key you selected, key #1, for one of the remaining keys, #3, #4, or #5. Do you make the swap?

Now let's see how you did in your probabilistic thinking. We'll assure you that the answers provided are correct, and we'll also assure you that barroom brawls have occurred because people won't accept the correct answers as being correct! For the math nerds reading this, we've included the mathematical solutions to all four problems in Appendix A.

For problem 1, most people will give a relatively low probability. Their thought process might be: there are 50 people in the room, there are 365 days in the year, and so the chances are 50 divided by 365, or around 14%. The reality is that with 50 people in a room, the odds are 97%! For person #1, there are 364 days that won't match. For person #2, there are 363 days that won't match, and so on. For there to be no match at all, every person must be a "no match." When you do the math, there is only a 3% chance of "no match" for everyone, so the chance that two people in the room share a birthdate is 97%.

For problem 2, most people will reason that since a gold coin is showing already, it can't be in the chest with two silver coins. Therefore, the chances are 50-50 of it being in the chest with two gold coins, so the chance of opening the other drawer and seeing a gold coin is 50%. This is seemingly logical, but incorrect. The correct answer is 2/3, or nearly 67%. Intuitively, when you eliminate the chest with two silver coins, there are three drawers left that have a gold coin – two in the gold-gold chest, one in the gold-silver chest. You don't know which one you are seeing, but of the three remaining drawers, there are two of them out of three that have a second gold in the other drawer – hence, a probability of 2/3, or nearly 67%!

For problem 3, many people will bet on black because "black is due." Again, that's faulty logic. If you assume that the wheel is fair, a red or a black is equally likely on the next spin, so it doesn't matter if you bet on red or black. If you assume that there is something flaky about the wheel since it came up red so many times and that the wheel is biased to come up red, you would bet on red. If the first assumption is correct, there is no reason not to bet on red. But if the second assumption is correct, there is a reason not to bet on black. Why not hedge your bets and bet on red!

For problem 4, most people will conclude that the remaining keys are equally likely to start the car, and they would feel terrible if they originally had the winning key and traded it for another. The reality is that the remaining keys are not equally likely. At the start, all keys were equally likely with a 1 in 5 or 20% chance of starting the car. After you've picked key #1, think of two "bins" of probability – the first bin with your selected key #1 having a 20% probability in it, and the other bin with the remaining four keys having an 80% probability split across four keys (20% each). The total probability in a bin doesn't change when the host gives you information about the other keys, but when he eliminates one of the keys, the 80% in the bin is now spread across three keys, so the probability for each of the remaining keys actually goes up! Bottom line – every time the host eliminates a key and offers you a trade, take it!

A Short Course in Thinking Probabilistically

Well, how did you do? If you are like most people, a short tutorial on how to think about uncertainty will be welcome.

So where do we start? Let's start with how we define probability which is a pretty universal measure of uncertainty. There are two schools of thought. The first is referred to as the classical approach and is widely used by statisticians. Probability is defined as the relative frequency with which an event will occur. That is, if you flip a coin 100 times and get 50 heads, you would say that the probability is 50 divided by 100, or 50%. It is viewed as a physical property of the coin. If you ask a classical statistician what the probability of a head on the next flip of a coin would be, the response would be "either 100% or 0%." One of the biggest shortfalls of the classical approach is that there are many uncertain events for which we have no relative frequency data. For example, what is the probability that Iran is conducting secret nuclear weapons research in an underground facility that the U.S. has not yet discovered? It is an important question to ask even though there may be little or no historical data on which to base relative frequencies. The classical approach leaves us with no way to address this.

The second approach to probability is referred to as the subjective probability approach, or the Bayesian probability approach, named for the Reverend Thomas Bayes who did the seminal work in the field. In this approach, probability is viewed as a state of information, or a state of mind. The probability of an event is based on all available information, to include relative frequency information (if available), expert judgment, elicited knowledge, etc. Here's an example. On your way into work, you are feeling a bit under the weather, and you decide to stop in at an Urgent Care Center to get checked out. While you are sitting in the waiting room, a middle aged man walks in and keels over on the floor. What is the probability that he has had a heart attack? You have little information, but you happened to have read an article that said that 1 in 10,000 men have heart attacks during their lifetime. Not a very good estimate for the man on the floor, but it is a starting point. You can see that the man is at least 100 pounds overweight, is holding his chest, and has a pack of cigarettes in his shirt pocket. Has your probability estimate of a heart attack changed? It probably has but not because the physical characteristics of the man writhing on the floor have changed. Rather, because your state of information has changed. Now, you overhear the nurse say that the man has crushing chest pain, pain in his left arm, smokes three packs of cigarettes a day, and has had three previous heart attacks! What about now, has your probability changed? We certainly hope so.

The key point here is that we want you to start thinking about probability in a new way. Start thinking as a Bayesian, and treat probability as a summary of all of the information that you know about an uncertain event. Don't be afraid to make your best estimate, even when there are little data available.

Now we need some basic understanding of probability terminology. This may be a bit painful for some of you but, if we are going to think probabilistically, we need to understand the basics. All probabilities must be on a scale that goes from 0% (which means you are absolutely certain that an event can't occur) to 100% (which means you are absolutely certain that an event will occur). 50% would mean that it is just as likely to occur as not. We call two uncertain events **mutually exclusive** if, when one outcome occurs, the other cannot occur. If the flip of a coin results in a head, it cannot be a tail, so heads and tails are mutually exclusive. When we describe the complete set of every outcome that occurs, we say that the outcomes are **collectively exhaustive**. For example, if you draw a card at random from a deck of cards and ask about the suit, the possible outcomes would be a heart, a club, a diamond, or a spade. Taken together, these outcomes are collectively exhaustive because they represent all possible outcomes. When all outcomes that occur are both mutually exclusive and collectively exhaustive, their probabilities must sum to 100%. When we discuss the probabilities of a single event happening, we call it a **marginal probability**. For example, the probability of pulling an Ace from a deck of cards is 4 out of 52, or roughly 8%. When we discuss the probability of two outcomes occurring together, we are talking about a **joint probability**. For example, we know that the probability of a card pulled from a deck being a spade is 13 out of 52, or 25% and, as indicated above, the probability of a card from a deck being an Ace is 4 out of 52, or roughly 8%. But the probability of pulling the Ace of spades (actually, two events happening together jointly) is only 1 out of 52, or roughly 2%. This probability is the joint probability of getting an Ace and getting a spade at the same time. The last term that we need to define is a **conditional probability**, or the probability of one outcome occurring *given* the fact that another outcome has already occurred. For example, the probability that the card you pulled is a spade given that it is an Ace is 1 out of 4, or 25%. The reason that it is important to understand the different types of probabilities is that the biggest mistakes that people make in interpreting probabilities is confusing conditional and joint probabilities, and reversing the order of events in a conditional probability. To illustrate this point, consider that the probability of getting lung cancer *given* that you are a smoker is actually very low, but the probability that you are a smoker *given* that you have lung cancer is very high. We can really come to incorrect conclusions if we don't understand these definitions.

It is also important to understand the language that we use in describing uncertainty and probabilities. We use a lot of words to describe uncertainty, and we don't use them in a common way. Think about the terms shown below. Knowing that probabilities must be between 0% and 100%, what probability would you associate with each of the following phrases?

- Is highly likely
- Could happen
- Is probable
- Is possible
- Is more likely than not

Here's an example that illustrates the problem we face in trying to communicate with each other on probabilities. In the early 1970s, the consulting firm that Terry later joined visited a military headquarters in Germany. At the time, a crisis was underway; there was a civil war in Jordan, with the Government forces fighting rebel Palestinian forces. The U.S. had many civilians there who were in danger, and the State Department was trying to decide whether to evacuate U.S. civilians. A cease fire had been declared, and the decision to evacuate hinged on how long we believed the cease fire would hold. The analysts from the consulting firm were given a report that stated "we believe that the cease fire *could* last up to 3 weeks." As experts in decision theory, the consultants were skeptical that this report conveyed the same information to all intelligence personnel who read it. They were told by one of the authors of the report that all analysts used a common language, and that the term could nominally represent the range of 20% to 40%, with a most likely probability of 30%. To test their skepticism, the consultants showed the report to a dozen analysts and asked them what probability the author of the report was trying to convey. As you might have guessed, the answers ranged from a low of 10% to a high of 90%! They questioned the analysts further, particularly those with more extreme assessments. When they questioned the analyst who responded 90%, they probed further by saying, "you might not have understood what we wanted; we didn't want your assessment, we wanted to know what the author was trying to convey." She looked them in the eye and said "no, you don't understand. I was a co-author of the report." I think the consulting firm made its point!

An interesting experiment was conducted years ago at an Intelligence Agency by a man named Sherman Kent in which trained intelligence analysts were asked to associate probabilities with words similar to those above. He expected a high degree of consistency, but found that assessments for the same terms were all over the place. As a result, training was changed, and all analysts are supposed to use the same probability scale as reflected in the chart shown below. [14] For expressions of likelihood or probability, an analytical product must use one of the sets of terms in the table below. Note that there is some intentional ambiguity since some probabilities such as 45% are at the limits of two different descriptions. There are also two different word descriptions for each probability range, one in each of the top two rows of the table.

Almost no chance	Very unlikely	Unlikely	Roughly even chance	Likely	Very likely	Almost certain
Remote	Highly improbable	Improbable	Roughly even odds	Probable	Highly probable	Nearly certain
01-05%	05-20%	20-45%	45-55%	55-80%	80-95%	95-99%

Unfortunately, no such common scale exists in the commercial world, but the Sherman Kent Scale above is a good starting place. Even with this scale, we'll have to deal with expressions such as "beyond a reasonable doubt" which can lead to unclear and inconsistent guidance as some of you may have faced in a courtroom as an attorney or as a juror.

> **Hot Tip:** *Never assign an extreme probability of 0% or 100% to anything! We don't always know what we don't know about a situation, and that can surprise us.*

USING PROBABILITY THEORY TO IMPROVE DECISIONS

But enough on probability theory itself; let's focus on how to use it to make better decisions!

Let's revisit our coin flip example by playing a betting game. If you call the next flip correctly, you win $10. If you call it incorrectly, you win nothing. We can represent your coin flip decision in what is known as a decision tree.

The small box to the left is called a **decision node**, and it shows our two choices for the decision: call "heads" or call "tails." The small circles are called **chance nodes,** and the branches coming out of them represent the **uncertain outcomes or possibilities**. In this case, the coin could be a head or it could be a tail. Under each potential outcome, we show the probability. Assuming a fair coin, this would be .5 or 50% for heads and .5 or 50% for tails. Along each path through the tree, we define the consequences. If you decide to call "heads" and heads comes up, you win. If it comes up tails, you lose. Associated with each consequence is a value. This value is interpreted in the same way as we did in the last chapter. In this case, if you win, you get $10, if you lose, you get nothing.

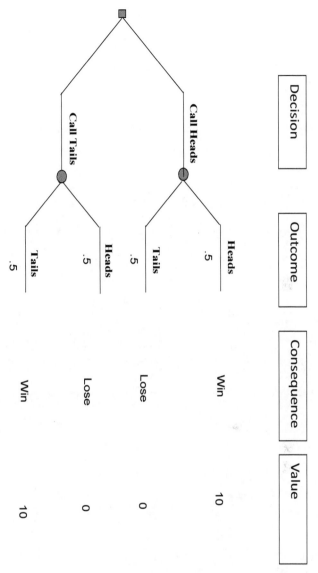

| Decision | Outcome | Consequence | Value |

Call Heads
- Heads .5 — Win — 10
- Tails .5 — Lose — 0

Call Tails
- Heads .5 — Lose — 0
- Tails .5 — Win — 10

Even if we perform no math with the tree, it provides us with a nice construct for thinking about the decision and laying out the sequence of thoughts and actions. But we can do some simple math that will help us to analyze the decision. There is a concept called **expected value** that is the combination of the probability of an outcome and the value associated with the outcome. At any decision node, we select

119

the choice with the highest expected value. At any chance node, we calculate the expected value by multiplying the probability and the value for each outcome at that node, and then add the results across all outcomes. In the example above, if you call "heads," there is a 50% chance of the coin coming up heads that would result in winning $10 and a 50% chance of the coin coming up tails that would result in winning $0. The expected value of the decision to call "heads" is then:

Expected value = .50 x $10 + .50 x $0 = $5

If we were to repeat this over and over, on the average, you would expect to win an average of $5 for each play. For the coin flip, the calculation would be the same if the decision were to call "tails." Ironically, even though we call this the expected value, we would never actually win $5 on any single coin flip. To overcome this confusion in terms, Keeney has suggested the term **contribution to overall desirability** rather than expected value. [15]

Simple decision trees can be used for virtually any decision, and we'll look at a few examples.

CASE STUDY: WHIPLASH! GO TO COURT VERSUS SETTLE – ANDREA MERLE, THE ATTORNEY

Andrea Merle is an attorney, and her client has been seriously injured in an automobile accident in which the other party was deemed to be at fault by the police officer at the scene. However, Andrea is concerned that the jury may believe that there was some contributory negligence on her client's part based on the police report. Assume that for this analysis, her comprehensive discussions with her client haven't shed any light on whether or not he could be accused of contributory negligence. Based on Andrea's experience, for the type of injury that her client has suffered, it would not be unusual for awards to be in the range of $50,000 to $350,000 if there is contributory negligence, and $250,000 to $1,500,000 if there is no contributory negligence. The insurance company for the other driver has offered her client a settlement of $400,000. She believes that it is equally likely that the jury will determine contributory negligence as not and, if it does, she believes that there is a 25% chance of a $200,000 award, a 50% chance of a $100,000 award, and a 25% chance of a $50,000 award. If the jury determines no contributory negligence, she believes that there is a 70% chance of a $1,000,000 award, a 20% chance of a $500,000 award, and a 10% chance of a $250,000 award. Her client is asking for her advice – settle, or go to court? (Assume that all awards are after attorneys' fees have been taken out.)

ANDREA'S DECISION TREE

We can model the uncertainty in the decision for Andrea's client with a simple decision tree. We start by arraying the data in simple matrices:

Jury Finding at Trial	Probability of Finding
Contributory negligence	50%
No contributory negligence	50%

Award	Probability of award	Average value of award
Settle	100%	$400,000
If contributory negligence		
Moderate	25%	$200,000
Low	50%	$100,000
Very low	25%	$50,000
If no contributory negligence		
Extremely high	70%	$1,000,000
Very high	20%	$500,000
High	10%	$250,000

We now use the data to develop the decision tree below. Andrea's primary decision for her client is to go to court or to settle for a certain $400,000. If she goes to court, there is a 50%-50% chance of the jury finding contributory negligence, and we show the uncertainty in the tree with a small circle (called a chance node) with two branches coming out of it, one for a finding of contributory negligence and one for a finding of no contributory negligence. We show the 50% probability for each below each branch. If the jury finds contributory negligence, there is additional uncertainty as to the size of the award. We represent that as another chance node and, for this example, we show three possible award levels and the probabilities that Andrea has assessed based on her experience with similar cases. The tree shows a similar chance node if there is a finding of no contributory negligence, but with different award levels and different probabilities.

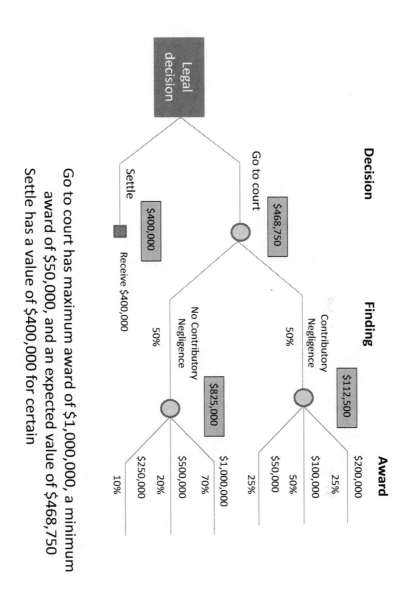

Decision		Finding		Award

Legal decision

Go to court — $468,750

Go to court has maximum award of $1,000,000, a minimum award of $50,000, and an expected value of $468,750

Contributory Negligence — 50% — $112,500
- $200,000 — 25%
- $100,000 — 50%
- $50,000 — 25%

No Contributory Negligence — 50% — $825,000
- $1,000,000 — 70%
- $500,000 — 20%
- $250,000 — 10%

Settle — $400,000 — Receive $400,000

Settle has a value of $400,000 for certain

In the same way that we calculated the expected value for our coin flip bet, we can do the same at each chance and decision node. This is known as **rolling back the decision tree**. For the awards for the contributory negligence case, there is a 25% chance of $200,000, a 50% chance of $100,000, and a 25% chance of $50,000. We can calculate the expected value as:

Expected value of award if there is a finding of contributory negligence =

.25 x $200,000 + .50 x $100,000 + .25 x $50,000 = $112,500

We show the $112,500 in the gray box above the chance node. Similarly:

Expected value of award if there is a finding of no contributory negligence =

.70 x $1,000,000 + .20 x $500,000 + .10 x $100,000 = $825,000

But now, we have to incorporate the probability that there will be a finding of either contributory negligence or no contributory negligence - a 50%-50% chance. That means there is a 50% chance of getting the previous expected value of $112,000 and a 50% chance of getting the $825,000. We then calculate the expected value of going to court as:

Expected value of going to court = .50 x $825,000 + .50 x $112,500 = $468,750.

We show this in the box over the "Go to court" branch. Now, we can see that if we settle, we can get $400,000 for certain. If we go to court, we can win a maximum of $1,000,000, a minimum of $50,000, and an expected value award of $468,750. Since this is higher than the certain $400,000, but has a risk of getting less, the client is in a good position to make a choice.

Many of you may be more comfortable doing the math in spreadsheets. Excel is pretty pervasive, and the problem setup for a spreadsheet is pretty simple. From the decision tree, we can see that that are seven possible combinations of events, or paths, through the tree, and we can represent that in the following table:

Decision Matrix for the Attorney's Client

Path #	(A) Choice	(B) Contributory negligence finding	(C) Award	(D) Probability of contributory negligence finding	(E) Probability of Award	(F) Probability of path = Column D x E	(G) Expected Award = Column C x F
1	Settle	-	$ 400,000	-	100%	100%	$ 400,000
2	Court	Yes	$ 200,000	50%	25%	12.5%	$ 25,000
3	Court	Yes	$ 100,000	50%	50%	25.0%	$ 25,000
4	Court	Yes	$ 50,000	50%	25%	12.5%	$ 6,250
5	Court	No	$ 1,000,000	50%	70%	35.0%	$ 350,000
6	Court	No	$ 500,000	50%	20%	10.0%	$ 50,000
7	Court	No	$ 250,000	50%	10%	5.0%	$ 12,500

Expected value of settling	$	400,000
Expected value of going to court	$	468,750

125

Column A shows that there is one path for settling and six paths for going to court. Column B shows that for the "go to court" paths, three represent a finding of contributory negligence and three do not. Column C shows the awards for each path. Column D shows the probability of a finding of contributory negligence for each path. Column E shows the probability of award amounts. Column F calculates the total probability for a path by multiplying together the probabilities along the path. Column G calculates the expected value for each path by multiplying the path probability by the award amount. We get the total expected value of award for going to court by adding up the expected values for all paths that are for going to court.

Using either the tree approach or the table approach, we can better understand and deal with the uncertainties that we will inevitably face.

ESTIMATING PROBABILITIES

An obvious question is "where do the probabilities for any problem come from?" The answer goes back to our definition of probability as the state of information that we have from all sources. In our litigious world, there are readily available experts (for hire!) on every topic imaginable. We have our own experiences with which to compare a new situation with something we've seen before. For medical problems, we can use a relative frequency approach since there are reams of data and databases that can connect symptoms with diseases. Still another approach is to assess a verbal definition of the probability of an event, for example, "highly likely." We can then use a pre-determined scale such as the Sherman Kent Scale described earlier to assign a probability. We can use an approach called reference processes in which we compare the probability of an event with a known probability. For example, Terry is a diehard Yankees fan, and if he wants to assess the probability that the Yankees will win the World Series next year, he can ask himself if that event is more or less likely than flipping a coin and getting "heads" – an event that has a known probability of 50%. Of course, he believes the Yankees' probability is greater than that (sorry, Red Sox fans!). Then he asks himself, is the probability for the Yankees greater or less than rolling a single die and getting anything other than a 1 – an event with a known probability of 5/6, or around 83%. Well, even a Yankees fanatic must believe that the Yankees' chances are less than that, so now he has the probability bracketed between 50% and 83%. By continuing in this fashion, he can narrow down the probabilities. In this case, he'll assess the Yankees' chances as 75%! Just for fun, here are some events and probabilities that can be used as reference processes [16]:

- Dying of a stroke   1/24
- Dying in a car accident in your lifetime   1/84
- Drowning in your lifetime   1/1,134
- Getting 10 heads in a row (coin flip)   1/10,000
- Getting a royal flush in poker   1/65,000
- Getting struck by lightning in your lifetime   1/80,000
- Getting killed by a shark in your lifetime   1/3,748,067

CASE STUDY: FLIP OR FLOP – MICHELE MICHAELS, THE REAL ESTATE INVESTOR

Michele Michaels is a real estate investor, and she is looking at a property to "flip" by trying to buy at a low price, make repairs, and sell at a nice profit within 90 days. Michele has a lot of experience flipping properties, and she has taken Omar Periu's course on *Real Estate Investing Made Easy*. Michele has several properties to consider, and she would like to think through the potential for one property in particular. It is a bank foreclosure that has been vacant for six months and it is being sold at a "sight unseen, as is" auction. She has done her due diligence and used the *Deal Flip Formula* template that she received in the course (see Appendix B) to gather the basic data that she will need. Michele has looked at comparable sales in the area and a realtor friend has given her an estimate of the appraised value after fix-up. Michele believes that if she can turn this house into an eye-catching fixer-upper, she will be able to sell it for $620,000. She has determined that the most that she is willing to offer for it is $450,000, and the opening bid has a minimum asking price of $375,000. Her experience tells her that most foreclosures in the neighborhood need at least $85,000 in rehab and upgrade costs. But she also knows that repairs may run as high as $125,000 if she discovers some unpleasant surprises such as asbestos, termites, or a nasty former owner who trashed the place. Michele has a realtor's license so she won't have to pay herself a commission upon resale, but the buyer's broker will get 2% of the sales price and closing costs will be 1% of the sales price. She intends to fund the purchase out of her own assets, so there will be no cost to acquire funds and holding costs should be negligible since she is anticipating a quick flip. Michele realizes that there is significant uncertainty in some of the estimates that she is using, and she wants to be able to deal with this uncertainty in a more sophisticated manner to answer the question "how much profit is she likely to make on this house if she decides to purchase it?"

Michele used the Deal Flip Formula and came up with the information on the next page:

Purchase Price	Probability of Purchase Price
$410,000	65%
$450,000	35%

Level of Repairs	Average Level of Repairs	Probability of Level of Repairs
$75,000 - $100,000	$85,000	55%
$100,000 - $135,000	$125,000	45%

Sales Price before broker commissions and closing costs	Sales Price after broker commissions and closing costs	Probability of Sales Price
$480,000	$465,600	10%
$550,000	$533,500	20%
$620,000	$601,400	70%

MICHELE'S DECISION TREE

Michele can now lay out the events as they would unfold and, even if she has no intention of doing the math, the decision tree presents a clear picture of the components of the decision. If Michele doesn't purchase, she makes nothing and lives to fight another day on another property. The first uncertainty is the amount she will have to spend to win the bid. For this example, she has shown two possible prices, $450,000 and $410,000, but she can expand the tree to include as many outcomes as she chooses. If she purchases the house, the next uncertainty is the amount of rehab and upgrades required. Again, she could have used as many possibilities as were needed to understand the decision. Her final uncertainty is the sales price of the property upon resale. Michele first uses adjectival descriptions such as high, medium, and low, but she then associates an actual sales price (after commissions and closing costs) with those words. For each path through the tree, at the far end, she shows the net profit if she ignores the uncertainties:

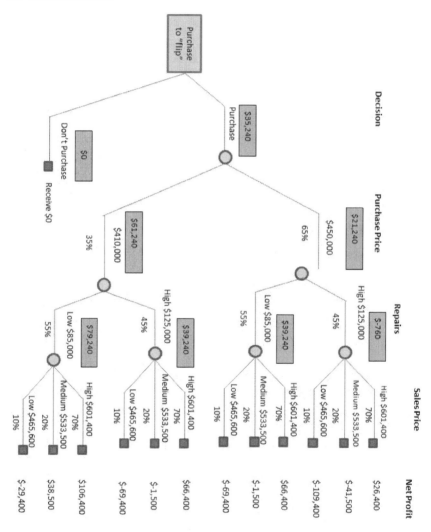

At this point, rather than rolling back the tree, Michele has decided to use the matrix approach in Excel to analyze the decision as shown below:

Decision Matrix for House Flip

Possible outcome #	(A) Purchase Price	(B) Probability of purchase price	(C) Repairs	(D) Probability of repairs	(E) Sale price	(F) Probability of sale price	(G) Net Profit for the outcome Columns E-(C+A)	(H) Probability of the outcome Columns BxDxF	(I) Expected profit of the outcome Columns GxH
1	$ 450,000	65%	$ 85,000	55%	$ 601,400	70%	$ 66,400	25.0%	$ 16,617
2	$ 450,000	65%	$ 85,000	55%	$ 533,500	20%	$ (1,500)	7.2%	$ (107)
3	$ 450,000	65%	$ 85,000	55%	$ 465,600	10%	$ (69,400)	3.6%	$ (2,481)
4	$ 450,000	65%	$ 125,000	45%	$ 601,400	70%	$ 26,400	20.5%	$ 5,405
5	$ 450,000	65%	$ 125,000	45%	$ 533,500	20%	$ (41,500)	5.9%	$ (2,428)
6	$ 450,000	65%	$ 125,000	45%	$ 465,600	10%	$ (109,400)	2.9%	$ (3,200)
7	$ 410,000	35%	$ 85,000	55%	$ 601,400	70%	$ 106,400	13.5%	$ 14,337
8	$ 410,000	35%	$ 85,000	55%	$ 533,500	20%	$ 38,500	3.9%	$ 1,482
9	$ 410,000	35%	$ 85,000	55%	$ 465,600	10%	$ (29,400)	1.9%	$ (566)
10	$ 410,000	35%	$ 125,000	45%	$ 601,400	70%	$ 66,400	11.0%	$ 7,321
11	$ 410,000	35%	$ 125,000	45%	$ 533,500	20%	$ (1,500)	3.2%	$ (47)
12	$ 410,000	35%	$ 125,000	45%	$ 465,600	10%	$ (69,400)	1.6%	$ (1,093)
								Expected Profit	$ 35,240

131

If all of the best outcomes happen together, she can make as much as $106,400 on the flip. If all of the worst things happen, she could lose $109,400. Considering all of the possible outcomes and their corresponding probabilities, her expected net profit is $35,240. It all comes down to how willing she is to accept the risk of a potential big loss as it balances out against the potential for a huge gain.

In both the legal and the real estate examples, we were able to use dollars as the value measure for determining how much we preferred one alternative over the other. As we saw in Chapters 4 and 5 on Choices and Consequences, there is more than one decision criterion and value needed for most decisions. In those cases, all we have to do is replace the dollar value measure in the decision tree with the overall value that we can calculate with our value hierarchy and, voila, we have a decision tree that can handle multiple and sometimes conflicting objectives. The math remains the same for rolling back the decision tree or performing calculations in a spreadsheet.

CASE STUDY: MIKE AND MADDIE – CAPTURING UNCERTAINTY IN A DECISION TREE

And now, it is time to check back in with Mike and Maddie. When we last left them, they had built consequence and value tables as shown on the next two pages:

Mike & Maddie's Consequence Table

Value measures	Choices (Score)	For Your Health	Fit To Be Tied	Better Bodies	Gym	Fitness Focus
Average same-chain annual return on investment	Score	52%		65%	77%	48%
Franchise 500 ranking	Score	None		60%	92%	85%
Miles to nearest same-chain competition	Score	No same chain close by		6	100	25
# of competing fitness franchises in zip code	Score	7		8	6	3
Level of corporate incentives	Score	Very high		Low	Low	High
Amount of state-of-the-art equipment	Score	None		A few	All	>50%
Variety and quantity of equipment	Score	Low		High	Very high	High
Breadth of services provided	Score	Training only		Training & marketing	All major 3rd-party	Training, accounting, marketing
Quality of services provided	Score	Don't know		High	Very high	Medium
Average same-chain annual staff turnover rate	Score	12%		<10%	15%	27%
Competitive compensation package	Score	Average market		Above market	Highly above market	Above market
Average hours per day spent at facility by same-chain franchisees	Score	10		6-8	12	6-8
Availability of affordable housing within 20 minutes	Score	High		High	Low	High
Requirements vs. Mike's financial situation	Score	Within financial resources		Doable, but will require financing	Borderline quality	Doable, but will require financing
Likelihood of obtaining required financing	Score	None needed		High	Medium	High
Initial capital contribution	Score	$75K		$110K	$250K	$190K
Annual royalty fee percentage	Scor	4%		5%	6%	5%
Length of lease (years)	Sco	5		4	1	6

133

Mike & Maddie's Value Table

Value measures	Choices	For Your Health	Fit To Be Tied	Better Bodies Gym	Fitness Focus
Average same-chain annual return on investment	Value	80	80	100	60
Franchise 500 ranking	Value	0	30	90	60
Miles to nearest same-chain competition	Value	100	67	100	100
# of competing fitness franchises in zip code	Value	20	20	20	50
Level of corporate incentives	Value	100	35	35	90
Amount of state-of-the-art equipment	Value	0	40	100	75
Variety and quantity of equipment	Value	0	80	100	80
Breadth of services provided	Value	0	60	100	85
Quality of services provided	Value	0	90	100	60
Average same-chain annual staff turnover rate	Value	67	100	67	33
Competitive compensation package	Value	60	85	100	85
Average hours per day spent at facility by same-chain franchisees	Value	35	90	10	90
Availability of affordable housing within 20 minutes	Value	85	85	35	85
Requirements vs. Mike's financial situation	Value	100	80	20	80
Likelihood of obtaining required financing	Value	100	90	60	90
Initial capital contribution	Value	100	80	80	80
Annual royalty fee percentage	Value	90	75	40	75
Length of lease (years)	Value	75	60	100	80
Total Value		1012	1247	1257	1358

Mike and Maddie Use a Decision Tree to Refine their Choice

Even though both Mike and Maddie felt comfortable with the tables, something still bothered Mike. On some of the value measures, even though he had given the choices a score, there was a lot of uncertainty in his mind about how the choices would *actually* score. In particular, he was concerned about using the average Return on Investment for the same chain. He realized that he needed to do a bit more analysis to ease his concerns. After Mike discussed this with Maddie, she gave Mike the go-ahead to revise the tables by himself based on his concerns since she believed that her interests were already built into what they had done previously.

Focusing on these two factors, Mike then builds the following table to summarize the assessments that he already had made in his value curves:

Choice	Average Same Chain Return on Investment	Value
For Your Health	52%	80
Fit To Be Tied	65%	80
Better Bodies Gym	77%	100
Fitness Focus	48%	60

He realizes that for his specific choices, the averages provide high-level insight, but don't capture the specifics of his situation. He believes that the key to high Returns on Investment is Customer Retention. Mike then builds the following decision tree to dig deeper:

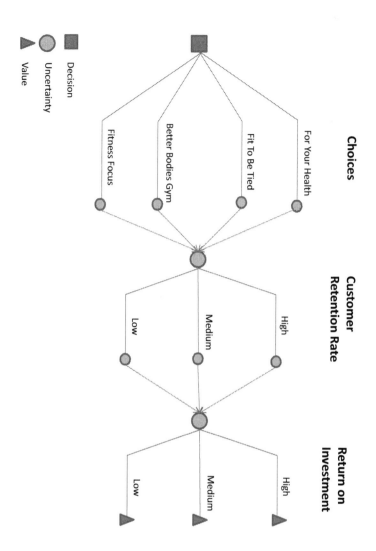

To keep the tree from getting too unwieldy to visualize, Mike shows that the Customer Retention chance node is attached to each choice, and that the Return on Investment uncertainty depends on which Customer Retention level is achieved. Since **For Your Health** is a relatively new franchise, Mike believes that there may be higher Customer Turnover. **Fit To Be Tied** has shown great Customer Retention rates, and he sees no reason why that shouldn't continue with his franchise. **Better Bodies Gym** has also done well on

Customer Retention, but Mike feels more uncertain about his prospects with the franchise. **Fitness Focus** has had problems with Staff Retention and that, in turn, has led to poor Customer Retention. Mike believes that if Customer Retention is high, there is also a high probability of strong Return on Investment. If Customer Retention is low, it will have a corresponding impact on Return on Investment. There are four franchise choices, three levels for Customer Retention, and three levels for Return on Investment. That means that there are 4 x 3 x 3 =36 possible paths through the tree. Mike decides to use the matrix approach to assess probabilities and to lay out the information as shown below. The table is read as follows: for the **For Your Health** choice, there is a 45% chance of Customer Retention being high, a 35% chance of it being medium, and a 20% chance of it being low. If Customer Retention is high, there is an 85% chance of Return on Investment being high, a 10% chance of it being medium, and a 5% chance of it being low. Any outcome that has a high Return on Investment, Mike values at 100; those with a medium Return on Investment are valued at 80; and those with a low Return on Investment are valued at 20. The table combines the probability of an outcome with the value of an outcome to calculate the expected value of Return on Investment. To get the expected ROI for an alternative, Mike just adds the expected values for all possible outcomes for the alternative.

Mike now has a better understanding of how the choices might do on Return on Investment, and he can use these expected values to replace the numbers in his earlier value matrix. He can easily see that **Fit To Be Tied** is highly valued at 90, **Better Bodies Gym** is not far behind at 84, **For Your Health** drops off to 78, and **Fitness Focus** is far lower at 49. By considering the uncertainties, Mike can better discriminate among the choices on a key factor, Return on Investment.

Outcome	Choices	Customer Retention	Customer Retention Probability	Return on Investment Score	Return on Investmentn Probability	Value associated with this outcome	Probability of this Outcome	Expected Value of this Outcome	Expected Value of Return on Investment
1	For Your Health	High	45%	High	85%	100	38%	38	
2	For Your Health	High	45%	Med	10%	80	5%	4	
3	For Your Health	High	45%	Low	5%	20	2%	0	
4	For Your Health	Med	35%	High	40%	100	14%	14	
5	For Your Health	Med	35%	Med	50%	80	18%	14	78
6	For Your Health	Med	35%	Low	10%	20	4%	1	
7	For Your Health	Low	20%	High	5%	100	1%	1	
8	For Your Health	Low	20%	Med	15%	80	3%	2	
9	For Your Health	Low	20%	Low	80%	20	16%	3	
10	Fit To Be Tied	High	85%	High	85%	100	72%	72	
11	Fit To Be Tied	High	85%	Med	10%	80	9%	7	
12	Fit To Be Tied	High	85%	Low	5%	20	4%	1	
13	Fit To Be Tied	Med	10%	High	40%	100	4%	4	
14	Fit To Be Tied	Med	10%	Med	50%	80	5%	4	90
15	Fit To Be Tied	Med	10%	Low	10%	20	1%	0	
16	Fit To Be Tied	Low	5%	High	5%	100	0%	0	
17	Fit To Be Tied	Low	5%	Med	15%	80	1%	1	
18	Fit To Be Tied	Low	5%	Low	80%	20	4%	1	
19	Better Bodies Gym	High	60%	High	85%	100	51%	51	
20	Better Bodies Gym	High	60%	Med	10%	80	6%	5	
21	Better Bodies Gym	High	60%	Low	5%	20	3%	1	
22	Better Bodies Gym	Med	30%	High	40%	100	12%	12	
23	Better Bodies Gym	Med	30%	Med	50%	80	15%	12	84
24	Better Bodies Gym	Med	30%	Low	10%	20	3%	1	
25	Better Bodies Gym	Low	10%	High	5%	100	1%	1	
26	Better Bodies Gym	Low	10%	Med	15%	80	2%	1	
27	Better Bodies Gym	Low	10%	Low	80%	20	8%	2	
28	Fitness Focus	High	10%	High	85%	100	9%	9	
29	Fitness Focus	High	10%	Med	10%	80	1%	1	
30	Fitness Focus	High	10%	Low	5%	20	1%	0	
31	Fitness Focus	Med	20%	High	40%	100	8%	8	
32	Fitness Focus	Med	20%	Med	50%	80	10%	8	49
33	Fitness Focus	Med	20%	Low	10%	20	2%	0	
34	Fitness Focus	Low	70%	High	5%	100	4%	4	
35	Fitness Focus	Low	70%	Med	15%	80	11%	8	
36	Fitness Focus	Low	70%	Low	80%	20	56%	11	

Incorporating Risk into the Decision

Before we move on, it is important to talk a bit about risk. For the purposes of this book, detailed risk modeling is an advanced topic that we won't cover, but we will introduce some of the basics. For those who want to learn more, we've identified some great reading material in the references section of this book.

So far, we are using a decision rule that says pick the choice with the highest expected value. For most of us though, that is only part of the story since that approach doesn't address risk. Let's start by defining what we mean by risk. According to the Society for Risk Analysis, risk is:

"The potential for realization of unwanted, adverse consequences..."

In practice, risk has two components: the likelihood of a bad thing happening, and the consequences if it does happen. In our everyday lives, we manage risk in several ways:

- **Risk avoidance** – we stay away from choices that can have severe negative results.

- **Risk transfer** – we buy insurance and pay for someone else to deal with very bad consequences (such as our auto insurance).

- **Risk mitigation** – we recognize that bad things do happen, and we prepare ourselves to deal with them when they occur.

Research shows that people have three attitudes towards risk. Some people are what we call risk neutral. They focus on expected value and tend to ignore the risk of potential downsides. Most of us are what we call risk averse - the expected value is part of the story, but we will avoid big risks even if the expected value looks promising.

The third attitude is what we call risk preferring - these folks will take chances far beyond what expected values would suggest. These are the people with whom you want to play poker!

Here is a simple example that illustrates the concept of risk attitude. You hold a raffle ticket with a 10% chance of winning $100,000 and a 90% chance of winning nothing. You paid nothing for the ticket. The expected value for the raffle is:

$$10\% \times \$100,000 + 90\% \times \$0 = \$10,000$$

If you played the raffle over and over again, on the average, you would expect to win $10,000 per play but, unfortunately, you only get to play it once.

What if someone offered to buy the raffle ticket from you? If that person offered you $1,000 for the raffle ticket, would you take the sure thing rather than the uncertain proposition? What if the offer were $7,500 – would you sell the raffle ticket? What if the offer were $20,000? If you are an expected value decision maker, the minimum you would accept is $10,000 since that is the expected value of the raffle. But most of us are risk averse, and we would accept an amount significantly less than the expected value of $10,000. That is the concept of risk attitude coming into play. And the important thing to recognize is that there is no correct choice here. The best answer for a homeless person living in a shelter would likely be very different than the answer for a millionaire. Even though this is a very simple, contrived example, when you think about it, this probably isn't a lot different than some decisions you've considered making when your buddy gave you some "hot tip" stock advice about a "can't miss" penny stock!

The bottom line is that you need to think beyond expected value and, even if you don't formally model risk, you need to include it in your thought process. Remember our real estate investor, Michele? If all of the best cases happen together, she can make as much as $106,400 on the flip. If all of the worst things happen, she could lose $109,400. Considering all of the possible outcomes and their corresponding probabilities, her expected net profit is $35,240. If all we looked at was expected value, Michele should buy the property since it has a reasonable expected return and, she may even stand to make $106,400. But there is also a significant downside, a possible loss of $109,400, and that is where the notion of risk comes into play. Perhaps Michele doesn't have the assets to withstand such a loss – that certainly will affect her decision.

There are some excellent software tools for doing probabilistic analysis. Our favorites include *DPL, @Risk, and Crystal Ball,* all of which are described in Appendix C.

At this point, we've made great progress in understanding how to frame our decision opportunities, how to specify our objectives, how to develop creative choices, how to measure consequences, and how to think about uncertainty. In the next chapter, we'll explore the kinds of swaps and trades that we usually have to make in every major decision.

RAPID RECAP: DEALING WITH UNCERTAINTY

- We need to view **probability as a state of information, or a state of mind**. The probability of an event is based on all available information, to include relative frequency information (if available), expert judgment, elicited knowledge, etc.

- We can use **decision trees** to portray our key uncertainties and to understand how our decisions unfold. The decision trees lay out our *choices*, our *possible outcomes*, our *probabilities* of the outcomes, our *consequences*, and the *values* of those consequences.

- The concept called **expected value** is the combination of the probability of an outcome and the value associated with the outcome. We can use expected value to compare choices.

- Our attitude towards **risk** should play a large role in our decision making. Risk is defined as "The potential for realization of unwanted, adverse consequences…" Risk has two components: the likelihood of a bad thing happening, and the consequences if it does happen.

- Most of us are **risk averse** decision makers; that is, we will select choices that reduce risk, even if expected values seem reasonable.

"As far as the laws of mathematics refer to reality, they are not certain; and as far as they are certain, they do not refer to reality."

~Albert Einstein

Chapter 7: Making Swaps and Trade-offs

"There are no solutions; there are only trade-offs."

~Thomas Sowell, *The Vision of the Anointed*

Up to this point, we've learned how to evaluate our choices in terms of our objectives and, most of the time, we are doing it in the face of an uncertain future. We've been able to develop value measures, we've created value scales for measurement, and we've captured probabilities about the uncertainties. In most of the important decisions that we make, there are multiple conflicting objectives. If we want a car with better gas mileage, we may have to give up some performance. If we want "more house" for our dollar, we may have to move further away from where we'd really like to be. If we want more return on our investment portfolio, we may have to take more risk. We typically Swap satisfaction of one objective for another by making trades. Sometimes this is easy, sometimes it is very challenging. Until now, we've ignored this critical concept. In this chapter, we'll learn to use some simple tools for prioritizing goals and objectives and making the relevant trades.

Hot Tip: *There are three basic truths about decision making:*
- *Some things are more important than others*
- *We usually can't get everything we want*
- *We often have to give up one thing to get another.*

As a way to get started, we can look at how one of our founding fathers, Benjamin Franklin, recommended making these kinds of trades. He had received a letter from a good friend, Joseph Priestly, asking for help in making a difficult decision. Most of us know the name Joseph Priestly as the scientist who is credited with discovering oxygen, although he was also a philosopher and theologian. Franklin didn't tell Priestly what to do but, rather, he told him how to go about making the choice. In Franklin's letter below, we have highlighted in bold the relevant information regarding trade-offs across objectives. Franklin wrote [17]:

Dear Sir,

In the affair of so much importance to you, wherein you ask my advice, I cannot, for want of sufficient premises, advise you what to determine, but if you please I will tell you how. When those difficult cases occur, they are difficult, chiefly because while we have them under consideration, **all the reasons pro and con are not present to the mind at the same time**, but sometimes one set presents themselves, and at other times another, the first being out of sight. Hence the various purposes or information that alternatively prevail, and the uncertainty that perplexes us. To get over this, my way is to **divide half a sheet of paper by a line into two columns; writing over one Pro, and over the other Con.** Then, during three or four days consideration, I put down under the different heads short **hints of the different motives, that at different times occur to me, for or against the measure.** When I have thus got them all together in one view, I endeavor to **estimate their respective weights; and where I find two, one on each side, that seem equal, I strike them both out.** If I find a reason pro equal to some two reasons con, I strike out the three. If I judge some

144

two reasons con equal to three reasons pro, I strike out the five; and thus proceeding I **find at length where the balance lies**. If after a day or two of further consideration, nothing new that is of importance occurs on either side, I come to a determination accordingly. And, though the weight of the reasons cannot be taken with the precision of algebraic quantities, **yet when each is thus considered, separately and comparatively, and the whole lies before me, I think I can judge better, and am less liable to make a rash step**, and in fact I have found great advantage from this kind of equation, and what might be called moral and prudential algebra.

Wishing sincerely that you may determine for the best, I am ever, my dear friend, yours most affectionately.

B. Franklin

Franklin, in his infinite wisdom, was able to help Priestly in a totally qualitative fashion. Often, that type of approach is all we need but, frequently, we'd like a more formal, analytical approach.

CASE STUDY: WENDI LEE – DEVELOPING WEIGHTS FOR TRADE-OFFS

Let's take a look at the simplified consequence and value matrices that we used for Wendi Lee's mobile computing decision earlier. (Note: in these matrices, the value measures are the rows and the choices are the columns - a perfectly acceptable way to form the matrices.) We scored each of the three choices on each of the four value measures, added up scores across the value measures, and calculated a total value for each choice as shown below. The value measures were considered to contribute equally to the decision, and no weights were used. The Microsoft SurfacePro 3 had the most points with 350.

Consequence Table	Choices		
Characteristics	MacBook Air	Dell Latitude 7000	Microsoft Surface Pro 3
Carrying weight (lbs.)	2.38	2.76	1.76
Battery life (hrs.)	9	7	8
Internal storage (Gigabytes)	526	128	256
Acquisition cost ($)	1099	1175	999

Value Table	Choices		
Characteristics	MacBook Air	Dell Latitude 7000	Microsoft Surface Pro 3
Carrying weight (lbs.)	40	30	100
Battery life (hrs.)	90	60	75
Internal storage (Gigabytes)	100	20	80
Acquisition cost ($)	70	40	95
Total value across characteristics	300	150	350
			⬆
			Best

After looking at the results, Wendi was bothered by something. As she thought about the problem, she realized that there really wasn't that much of a difference in the costs from the cheapest to the most expensive choice, and that the carrying weights of the devices themselves didn't vary by much. The difference in battery life meant a lot to her since she frequently traveled cross country.

Somehow, she had to incorporate these issues into the decision-making process.

The good news is that she can easily solve this problem by assigning numerical weights to the objectives and value measures to reflect their relative importance. This is one of the most commonly used practices in performing these types of analyses but, unfortunately, it is a practice that is frequently done improperly.

Let's look at two different approaches that people use when making swaps across the value measures. The first uses **importance weights**. To get them, we ask the question "How important is measure A versus measure B?" We can ask Wendi to compare the importance of carrying weight, battery life, internal storage, and acquisition cost. Assume that she first puts them in the following rank order: carrying weight, acquisition cost, battery life and internal storage. Next, we ask her to make some relative comparisons. Later, we'll talk about various weighting techniques but, for now, we'll use a simple approach of assigning 100 importance weight points to the value measures in proportion to their relative importance. For example, let's say Wendi assigns 50% of the points to carrying weight, 25% of the points to acquisition cost, 15% of the points to battery life, and 10% of the points to internal storage. We interpret these to mean that carrying weight is equally as important as the other three measures combined (50 points vs. 50 points), carrying weight is twice as important as acquisition cost (50 points vs. 25 points), acquisition cost is equal in importance to battery life and internal storage combined (25 points vs. 25 points), etc. We can make these judgments because our weights are on a ratio scale as we described earlier. Now, instead of just adding the values across value measures for each choice, we apply the importance weight percentage for each value measure by multiplying it by the value on each measure, and then adding them across all measures. For example, for the MacBook Air, the total value would be:

Total Value of MacBook Air = .

50 x 40 + .15 x 90 + .10 x 100 + .25 x 70 = 61

By making the importance weights add to 100% and by using a value scale from 0 to 100, we have the added benefit of putting the overall results on a 0 to 100 scale that makes them easier to interpret. The revised table would look like the following:

Weighted Value Table		Choices		
Characteristics	Importance Weights	MacBook Air	Dell Latitude 7000	Microsoft Surface Pro 3
Carrying weight (lbs.)	50%	40	30	100
Battery life (hrs.)	15%	90	60	75
Internal storage (Gigabytes)	10%	100	20	80
Acquisition cost ($)	25%	70	40	95
Total value across characteristics		61	36	93
				⬆
				Best

Note that the Microsoft SurfacePro 3 is still the highest scoring choice, but the MacBook Air and the Dell Latitude 7000 have gotten much closer together and are far lower than the SurfacePro.

Now that we've taken the trouble to go through the importance weight approach, we are going to tell you that this is the most commonly used approach and that *this is the wrong way to do it!*

Instead of using importance weights, we really want to use what are known as **swing weights** which have two components – the importance of the value measure *and* the size of the gap between the top and the bottom of the value scale. In essence, we are measuring the importance of the swing from the bottom to the top of the scale, hence the name swing weights.

Let's illustrate the idea of swing weights with Wendi's decision. Even though acquisition cost is important to her, there is only a $176 difference between the best and worst alternatives, and she finds that pretty insignificant. Similarly, even though carrying weight is also important to her, the difference between 1.76 lbs. and 2.76 lbs. is minor. On the other hand, the two-hour difference in battery life could be critical for her cross-country trips and, of the four value measures, this is the most significant swing in capability. She also has some memory intensive applications programs, so the differences in internal storage are an important part of her decision. Wendi judges that the difference in battery life is equally important as all of the other three differences combined. She believes that the difference in internal storage is more than twice as important as the differences in carrying weight and acquisition cost combined. Finally, she believes that differences in acquisition cost are twice as important as differences in carrying weight. To reflect these judgments, Wendi assigns 50% of the swing weight to battery life, 35% to internal storage, 10% to acquisition cost, and 5% to carrying weight as shown in the table below:

Weighted Value Table		Choices		
Characteristics	Swing Weights	MacBook Air	Dell Latitude 7000	Microsoft Surface Pro 3
Carrying weight (lbs.)	5%	40	30	100
Battery life (hrs.)	50%	90	60	75
Internal storage (Gigabytes)	35%	100	20	80
Acquisition cost ($)	10%	70	40	95
Total value across characteristics		89.0	42.5	80.0
		↑		
		Best		

The calculations for total value are done in the same manner as before:

Total Value of MacBook Air = .05 x 40 + .50 x 90 + .35 x 100 + .10 x 70 = 89

Total Value of Dell Latitude = .05 x 30 + .50 x 60 + .35 x 20 + .10 x 40 = 42.5

Total Value of SurfacePro 3 = .05 x 100 + .50 x 75 + .35 x 80 + .10 x 95 = 80

Recall that when she made the mistake of using importance weights, the SurfacePro 3 appeared to be the best alternative. When she uses swing weights, the best choice now is the MacBook Air, and this better reflects her preferences.

TECHNIQUES FOR DEVELOPING SWING WEIGHTS

There are many techniques we can use to assess the swing weights, but for our purposes, we will only discuss a few of the easiest to apply. The first is the one we used in Wendi's example – spread 100% of the weight across the value measures. Think of the process as having 100 coins that you can allocate to the swings in the value measures. A value measure that gets 50 coins has twice the swing in value than another value measure that gets 25 coins since we are using a ratio scale. A second technique is to directly assess the ratios from value measure to value measure. Start by rank ordering the swings in value measures; next, assign a weight of 100 to the highest ranked swing, and assign numbers to the other swings that reflect the ratios. The nice thing about this approach is that we are not constrained to make the assessments initially add up to 100%. Using this approach, Wendi would assign a 100 to her most significant swing, battery life. Compared to the 100, she believes the swing in internal storage should be around a 70. Finally, she assigns swing weights of 20 and 10 to acquisition costs and carrying weight respectively. Next, she adds up all of the points she assigned (200 in this case), and then she divides each assessed weight by the sum. This is called normalization, and it forces the final weights to add up to 100% as shown in the table above.

A somewhat more sophisticated approach, but still relatively easy to use, is called the swing weight matrix in which, rather than trying to assess the two components of a swing in one assessment, we rate the value measures on each component separately:

		Importance of the Value Measure		
		High	Medium	Low
Size of the Swing	High			
	Medium			
	Low			

We discuss the nature of the swings for each value measure, put each value measure in the appropriate box, assign a weight of 100 to the most significant cell at the top left, and assign other weights in terms of their relationship to that cell.

Wendi first assigns each of the value measures to a cell in the matrix, sets her most significant swing weight, battery life, to 100, and assigns weights to the other value measures relative to battery life. For Wendi, the swing weight matrix would look like the following:

		Importance of the Value Measure		
		High	Medium	Low
Size of the Swing	High	Battery Life 100		
	Medium	Internal storage 70		
	Low		Cost 20	Carrying weight 10

Once again, we would normalize the weights to sum to 100% by adding all of the weights and dividing each by the total. Any of the above techniques can work well as long as, when we ask the weighting questions, we always ask them to get swing weights, not importance weights.

CASE STUDY: MIKE AND MADDIE – DEVELOPING SWING WEIGHTS AND EXPLORING SWAPS

It is time to revisit Mike and Maddie. Earlier, we looked at Mike and Maddie's value matrix and, to evaluate the choices, we added all of the values for a choice across all of the value measures to get a total score. But by doing that, we made a fundamental assumption that every value measure was equally important and carried just as much influence in determining the overall value as any other value measure. In general, this is one of the worst assumptions that we can make in our decision making. If everything is important, then nothing is important. Remember Pareto's Rule: we can state a variant of it as 20-30% of the factors in a value model will usually account for 70-80% of what is important. Mike now realizes that all objectives and value measures are not equally important; he understands that he must consider not only the importance of the measures, but the significance of the difference between the worst and best choice on each value measure.

Mike's first step is to develop his swing weight matrix:

Mike's Swing Weight Matrix

		Importance of the Value Measure		
		High	**Medium**	**Low**
Size of the Swing	**High**	Average same-chain annual ROI Average same-chain annual staff turnover rate	Franchise 500 ranking Level of corporate incentives Initial capital contribution Breadth of services provided	Length of lease (years) Miles to nearest same-chain competition
	Medium	Requirements vs. Mike's financial situation Variety and quantity of equipment	Likelihood of obtaining required financing Annual royalty fee percentage	Competitive compensation package
	Low	Amount of state-of-the-art equipment Quality of services provided	Availability of affordable housing within 20 minutes	Average hours per day spent at facility by same-chain franchises # of competing fitness franchises in zip code

He then replaces his original value measure for Average Same-Chain Return on Investment (ROI) by the Expected ROI that he calculated using his decision trees, and he then eliminates the value measures for the Breadth of Services Provided, Quality of Services Provided, Amount of State-of-the-Art Equipment, and Variety and Quantity of Equipment since they were already captured in his probabilistic analysis of Customer Retention.

He then decides that he could get most of what he needs by using a smaller subset of the value measures (as per Pareto!), and he eliminates several of the measures that were in the lower right and adjacent cells of the swing weight matrix. He uses the method of assigning a swing weight of 100 to the most significant value measure and weighting the others in relationship to that measure and to each other. For example, the swing in Expected ROI is judged to be twice as important as the swing in Financial Requirements, so swing weights of 100 and 50 are assigned respectively to reflect this judgment. The swing in Financial Requirements is judged to be five times as important as the swing in Length of Lease, hence, weights of 50 and 10 are assigned. Once all relative swing weights are determined, Mike then adds the weights together, divides each by the total, and forces the weights to add up to 100% for ease in interpretation. The reduced set of the value measures and their weights are shown below:

Mike's Revised Value Measures and Swing Weights		
Value Measure	Assigned Weight	Weights Add to 100%
Expected ROI	100	29.0%
Average same-chain staff turnover rate	70	20.3%
Financial requirements vs. Mike's financial situation	50	14.5%
Initial capital contribution	35	10.1%
Franchise 500 ranking	25	7.2%
Likelihood of obtaining financing	20	5.8%
Annual royalty percentage fee	15	4.3%
Length of lease	10	2.9%
Level of corporate incentives	10	2.9%
Competitive compensation package	5	1.4%
Availability of affordable housing within 20 minutes	5	1.4%

To put all of the pieces together, Mike then updates his value table to include the results of his uncertainty analysis, his reduction in the number of the key value measures, some tweaking of values based upon some additional research, and his swing weighting to produce the revised value table as shown below:

Mike's Value Table

Value measures	Swing Weights	For Your Health (Value)	Fit To Be Tied (Value)	Better Bodies Gym (Value)	Fitness Focus (Value)
Expected ROI	29.0%	78	90	84	49
Franchise 500 Ranking	7.2%	0	45	90	60
Level of corporate incentives	2.9%	100	45	35	90
Average Same-Chain Annual Staff Turnover Rate	20.3%	60	100	67	33
Competitive Compensation Package	1.4%	60	85	100	85
Availability of Affordable Housing Within 20 Minutes	1.4%	85	85	35	85
Requirements Vs. Mike's Financial Situation	14.5%	100	80	20	80
Likelihood of Obtaining Required Financing	5.8%	85	95	60	90
Initial Capital Contribution	10.1%	100	80	80	80
Annual Royalty Fee Percentage	4.3%	85	75	40	75
Length of Lease (Years)	2.9%	75	65	100	80
Total Value		**75**	**84**	**67**	**61**

Note that his top four value measures in terms of swing weights account for approximately 36% of the value measures (4 out of 11) and 74% of the swing weight - right in line with what Pareto would have predicted! To fully understand each alternative, Mike then multiplies the swing weight on a value measure by the value of the alternative on that value measure, and adds across all value measures to get the column labeled Total Value.

Recall that, originally, when all value measures were treated as equally important, **Fitness Focus** had the highest value. But when Mike put increased emphasis on Expected ROI and Staff Turnover Rate, **Fitness Focus** dropped significantly and **Fit To Be Tied** has now emerged as Mike's best choice with a value of 84 out of a possible 100. **Fit To Be Tied** offers the highest expected ROI, is great in terms of low Staff Turnover Rate and Customer Retention, and its Initial Capital Contribution is compatible with their financial situation and ability to borrow money – all of the things that matter most to Mike and Maddie. **For Your Health** also looks like a viable alternative, only a few points behind **Fit To Be Tied**. It is better on the financial value measures but not as good on ROI and on Staff Turnover. As Mike and Maddie dig deeper and review the results more carefully, they feel pretty good about them and, intuitively, they make sense. Mike takes a deep breath, turns to Maddie, and says "Looks like we're **Fit To Be Tied!**" Maddie responds, "I'm on board with the decision. Now it is time to start making it happen."

> **Hot Tip:** *When a decision maker tells you that two alternatives are equally valued and that she can't choose between them, tell her that you are going to flip a coin to pick the "winner" and that she will have to accept the results. The decision maker's reaction to the result of the flip will tell the decision maker if the alternatives were really equal.*

FRANCHISING POST SCRIPT FROM OMAR

The fitness franchising example used throughout the book is near and dear to my heart. I owned and operated a health club for many years and if you'll pardon the pun, the operation was in good health and great shape. The opportunity to expand by adding additional clubs was very real and achievable. The choice I faced, however, was a challenge. Should I buy into an existing franchise or start my own brand? The franchise option seemed the best deal – until I looked into it and a study of the fine print that went along with the option.

After a lot of research and soul-searching, I chose to expand by owning and operating my own clubs under my own brand. Why?

The two biggest deciding factors were economics and control. I had approached an established and successful firm about franchising and in short order got a crash course in the two factors I just mentioned. Buying a franchise required an enormous upfront payment – something in the neighborhood of $350,000. That's just to get in the game. After I purchased the franchise rights I would have to pay the organization a whopping 24 % of my franchise income for as long as I owned the franchise. If you've ever owned a business you realize the impact of saying goodbye to nearly a quarter of your profits right off the top every quarter, ever year, every decade – forever. Additionally, as a franchisee, I would have to manage my business under their strict and very detailed set of rules, regulations and procedures. In essence, *they* would be running *my* business. Their one-size-fits-all approach to management worked well for their company, but would have put a straight-jacket on me as to how I'd run my operation. The way I looked at it then was that the business would be mine in name only and that name wouldn't even be the one over the door.

RAPID RECAP: SWAPS AND TRADE-OFFS

- In most major decisions, there are three basic truths:
    - Some things are more important than others
    - We usually can't get everything we want
    - We often have to give up one thing to get another.

- We incorporate these truths into our decision making by prioritizing and weighting our value measures.

- A best-practice weighting process is to use swing weights which reflect both the importance of the value measure and the significance of the difference between the worst case and best case possible on each value measure.

- Using importance weights instead of swing weights and ignoring the range in each value measure is one of the biggest mistakes that people make in decision making. It can significantly skew your results in a negative way.

- We get the total value for an alternative by multiplying the swing weight on a value measure by the value of the alternative on that value measure, and adding across all value measures.

"Strategy is about making choices, trade-offs; it's about deliberately choosing to be different."

~Michael Porter, *Strategic Planning Expert*

NOTES:

Chapter 8: Selecting Solutions

"There are no problems, only solutions."

~John Lennon, *The Beatles*

"Identify your problems, but give your power and energy to solutions."

~Tony Robbins, *Motivational Speaker*

We've spent the last seven chapters teaching you how to be a **FOCCUSSED** decision maker, and we've provided an analytic roadmap of how to think about your most challenging decision problems and opportunities. In this chapter, we need to spend a little time talking about the end game of the process – the Solution. There are three basic concepts that we want you to take away with you:

1. We have focused on the analytical, or technical side of the decision-making process. Unless we also recognize that decision making is a "socio-technical" process, we will rarely be able to carry our solutions to fruition.

2. We should always look at what appears to be the best solution and see if we can make it better.

3. We need to know when to stop analyzing and to start implementing solutions.

We'll address each of these in turn.

Decisions as Socio-Technical Processes

As a young engineer, Terry was very much enthralled with finding the "optimal solution" to problems and opportunities. It took a long time for him to realize that finding sound analytical solutions was only part of the task. A colleague of his who is a noted decision analyst, Dr. Larry Phillips, finally convinced him that decision making is a "socio-technical" process. [18] By that, we mean that we must consider not only the correct *analytical* solution (the technical side of the process), but equally important are the social and psychological aspects surrounding our decisions (the "socio" side of the process). Over the years, we have seen many technically sound analyses sit unused because they ignored things such as the style of the decision maker, the cultural aspects of the organization for which the decision was made, the intuitive aspects of the decision-making process, the influence of minor stakeholders, and the practical aspects of implementing the solutions.

In reality, making great decisions without planning for their implementation is a sure-fire way of ensuring failure. Unfortunately, most people wait until after the decision is made to start thinking about implementation. If we want to increase the chances of a good decision, we need to get the implementers involved right from the start. Implementers are one of the most important classes of stakeholders, and not involving them up front can be a critical mistake leading to what appear to be very innovative solutions that can never happen. Steven Covey, in *The 7 Habits of Highly Effective People,* cites habit 2 as "Begin with the End in Mind." [19] This applies equally well to getting all stakeholders involved from the start as it does to how we will communicate the results of our decision-making processes.

Five barriers to involving the implementers at the start of the process are described in the *Handbook of Decision Analysis* [20]:

1. The culture of the enterprise making the decision may not be willing to get the implementers involved.

2. It may be difficult to identify the ultimate implementers who may change over time. This is particularly true in the Government setting where people rotate jobs fairly frequently.

3. Implementers may be swamped with near-term tasks and may be unwilling to get involved in longer-term problems. They often believe that they can "come up to speed later."

4. For some decision opportunities, the stakeholders are in different physical locations, and the implementers may be quite a distance from the decision makers.

5. In many cases, the people analyzing or even making the decisions may have little experience in implementing solutions. This may leave them in the dark as to what questions to ask and as to how to analyze the implementation process itself.

Experience has shown that the best way to overcome these barriers is to include implementation concerns in each step of the **FOCCUSSED** decision-making process. We do this by including the implementers as key stakeholders right from the start, keeping them engaged as the process unfolds, and communicating regularly with them to ensure and enable their commitment to the process. For example, it is particularly helpful to involve stakeholders and implementers in:

- Drafting the vision statement

- Framing the key issues and identifying stakeholders

- Reviewing the strategy table

- Reviewing choices to be considered

- Identifying and evaluating value measures

- Conducting swaps and trades

- Gathering data.

GENERATING BETTER SOLUTIONS
THAN THE APPARENT "BEST SOLUTION"

Even many **FOCCUSSED** decision makers get caught in the trap of accepting what appears to be the best of the choices that came out of the decision-making process. They've considered the objectives, the consequences, and the uncertainties and have identified the highest valued choice. But we need to remember what we discussed in the chapter on Choices – if we have nothing but inferior choices to evaluate, we will only discover the best of the bad choices. That is why the **FOCCUSSED** decision-making process is an iterative approach. When we get to the end of the first pass at evaluation, we need to ask "are there ways to improve upon the best choice?" As was suggested earlier, one way of doing this is to always include an "ideal" alternative that would be valued at 100 on every value measure. We can then compare the choice that was best in the evaluation to the ideal alternative. The goal is to identify characteristics of the best choice where we scored lower than the ideal alternative, particularly, on value measures that carried high swing weights and had a large effect on the decision. We then attempt to craft an improved choice that scores better in areas for which the best choice left a lot of points on the table. Sometimes, all it takes is a little tweaking of the choice. Other times, the best approach is to create a hybrid choice that may combine the best features of several of the original choices. For example, if we have evaluated a set of new automobile choices for purchase, and if our best choice across all value measures scores low on fuel economy and environmental impact, a light bulb may come on that tells us that perhaps an electrical hybrid version of the same car will fare far better in terms of our objectives.

This notion of iteration is particularly important if our decision-making process involves a group of stakeholders. Over the years, we've discovered that it is best to build an evaluation model quickly and see what the initial results tell us. If all heads in the room are nodding in agreement, we get really worried. It is extremely difficult to capture all of the elements of the decision correctly the first time, partially because many people have hidden agendas that will only be uncovered if the decision doesn't go their way.

Hot Tip: *People generally have two very good reasons for doing something: the reason that they talk about and the reason that they keep to themselves. [21]*

Since most problems have conflicting objectives, we look for disagreement early in the process to identify the most contentious issues, encourage extensive discussion and debate on those issues, and then revise the initial models as we reconcile the issues through discussion.

Hot Tip: *As a rule of thumb, it is better to have stakeholders discuss and argue over the **results** rather than over **every single input** to the model.*

The bottom line – we should build and analyze decision models quickly, identify and reconcile areas of disagreement, and develop improved choices that better meet our objectives.

Knowing When to Stop Analyzing and to Start Implementing

It is a natural tendency to be concerned that we have left something critical out of our decision-making process. We need to talk to more people, we need to do more due diligence, we need to gather more data, etc. For some people, this is a defense mechanism that keeps them from finally having to make a decision; it is a delaying tactic because they are afraid that they'll make the wrong decision. They'd sooner avoid making a decision than risk a bad outcome. But, unfortunately, the "do-nothing" choice is also a very real choice whether we mean it to be or not. That is why it is essential to know when to stop analyzing and when to get on to making the decision. We stop modeling when we have created what is known as a **requisite decision model**. According to Larry Phillips, a requisite decision model is defined as a model whose form and content are sufficient to solve a particular problem. [22]

Basically, that means we should only model what is needed to solve the problem (or, in our case, to select the best choice), and nothing more. Unfortunately, it is not always easy to know when we have achieved this situation. But one thing is clear from years of experience in helping people to make good decisions - we have some good guidelines as to when to stop our modeling efforts and get down to the business of making things happen by considering the following ideas:

- Perfection is the enemy of good enough; this is often attributed to the author Voltaire who said "the perfect is the enemy of the good." [23]

- Remember what we learned earlier from Pareto, that 20-30% of our inputs can result in 70-80% of what we need.

- Ockham's razor (or in Latin, "lex parsimoniae," which means "law of parsimony") is a problem-solving principle devised by philosopher and theologian William of Ockham. The principle states that "among competing hypotheses that predict equally well, the one with the fewest assumptions should be selected." Other variations of this include "The simplest explanation for some phenomenon is more likely to be accurate than more complicated explanations," and "If you have two equally likely solutions to a problem, choose the simplest." [24]

Hot Tip: *In analyzing decisions, we generally have to balance defensibility in terms of theory, and practicality in terms of constrained analytical resources.*

To summarize, Terry has compiled a list of barriers based upon his experiences over the last 40 years in making and implementing good decisions as follows:

1. **Inadequate problem framing** – We frequently over-constrain or under-constrain the problem statement, thus leading to alternatives that don't really make sense, or we eliminate alternatives prematurely. An example of this was the inadequate problem framing of the "mechanical tomato picker" that we discussed earlier.

2. **Decision paralysis** by waiting for "all of the data" – We frequently fail to finish our work because we continually search for more data. The reality is that it is rare that "all" the data are available, and it is more effective to use a "requisite" approach to data gathering – gather what is needed to make the decision and no more.

3. **Looking for a 100% solution** – We have to know when to stop thinking about a problem. In the same way that the

notion of requisite data gathering was described above, a requisite decision model is one with adequate form and content to resolve the most important issues at hand.

4. **Ineffective group decision making processes** –Too often, we assume that making group decisions with others is automatically better than individual decision processes. This view has been magnified with the advent of group-enabling software such as *Go-To-Meeting, Meeting Works, Meeting Sphere*, etc. Such software manufacturers often tout the advantage of the anonymity that is provided to increase willingness to participate. However, anonymity can actually weaken the group process by providing a shield to hide behind in allowing participants to remain fixed in their views rather than increasing an open exchange of information.

5. **Lack of access to the decision maker**– For most of the cases we've discussed, the entrepreneur is the sole decision maker but, there are times when we are making or recommending decisions with or for others. The financial planner needs to understand clients' objectives and attitudes towards risk, but the client must live with the potential losses; the attorney knows the law, but the client lives with the consequences of the legal strategy decisions; the doctor knows the probabilities of diseases and outcomes, but the patient must live with the results and is the ultimate decision maker; etc. All too often, the people carrying out the steps of **FOCCUSSED** decision making don't seek or get to query the actual decision maker. This is essential to properly frame the problem and to understand the preferences essential for value-focused thinking. In all of these cases, it is really important to meet with the decision maker as early and as often as possible without wasting his or her valuable time.

6. **Insensitivity to deadlines and the effects of time** – We often get so enraptured with the cleverness of our decision-making thought processes that we lose sight of the decision timelines. For example, in trying to evaluate the best option for refinancing a mortgage, if you take too long to decide, the rates may go up and you get locked out of what was previously the best decision. If you delay a decision on long-term care or disability insurance, your health may change for the worse and render you uninsurable. It is essential that your decision-making processes be "designed to time" so as to be responsive to time-sensitive events. A timely 80% solution is usually better than a 100% solution that is too late.

7. **No plan to implement the decision** –It is essential to have a workable plan to implement the solution that is produced by the decision-making process. An analytically "correct" alternative that can't be executed within time, dollars, or other constraints is of little use to us.

Case Study: Mike and Maddie – A Re-look Leads to a Better Decision

Now, before we end this Chapter, we need to take a final look at Mike and Maddie. When we last saw them, they had completed their evaluation and had selected **Fit To Be Tied** as their best choice for a fitness industry franchising opportunity and were ready to start making it happen.

Mike was pretty happy and decided to tell his best friend, Ryan Jackson, about his plans. He knew that Ryan was a serious gym rat, and he figured that Ryan would be glad to celebrate Mike's decision to get into the fitness game over a couple of beers. Mike told Ryan the news, and Ryan thought that the idea was great.

"Mike, I had no idea that you were even considering this," said Ryan. "You should have talked to me though – before I moved here and met you, I actually managed a small fitness center in Delaware. It was a real kick, and I only left it because my wife, Joy, who was my fiancée at the time, had a great job down here in her family business. Her Dad offered me a job as well. I took it, but I kind of miss the old job. What made you pick the franchise that you did?"

Mike explained his **FOCCUSSED** decision process to Ryan, and Ryan thought that it was a neat way to make a decision. Mike explained about the objectives, and told Ryan how **Fit To Be Tied** hit some of his hot buttons. The expected ROI looked promising, average staff turnover for the chain was low, and the cash and net worth requirements were well within Mike's financial situation. Ryan then asked Mike an interesting question. "What don't you like about the choice you made, Mike?" Mike hesitated for a minute, and then thought about his value matrix. Mike replied, "The corporate incentives for new members were pretty bad, the chain didn't have a great rating with Franchise 500, the royalty fees were high, and they wouldn't commit to a long term lease. But the franchise still rated better than the other alternatives."

Ryan stared at Mike for a few seconds, and then asked: "Mike, did you ever consider starting your own gym instead of going with an existing franchise? I almost did that years ago, but Joy thought it would be far better to move here near her family and I just caved. Mike replied, "No, I never considered it, but now that you mention it, it does sound intriguing – though risky."

They continued to throw the idea around over a couple of beers, and Ryan surprised Mike with the idea that he would be interested in working for Mike and managing a gym full time if Mike started his own fitness facility. After all, Ryan had experience and, even better, Ryan said that he knew some really great personal trainers and other folks who would be terrific employees at a new gym. Not only that, he knew of a small privately-owned gym whose owner had become quite ill and was looking to sell all of his equipment and get out of the business since he couldn't manage it any longer. Mike thought about Ryan's proposal in terms of his value hierarchy. On the plus side, the potential for a really high ROI was there, but he still had to run some probabilistic projections to support his gut feeling. If Ryan was right about the equipment for sale and about the trainers, Staff Turnover would be low and Customer Retention would be high since they could open a high-quality facility. He could create his own compensation package and could run things the way he wanted. And there would be no royalty fees to siphon off profits. With Ryan as the full-time manager, Mike could see himself transitioning away from having to be on site full time – something that Maddie would like. On the down side, there would be no corporate support for third- party functions, but Ryan said that those types of services could easily be purchased directly, even though they might be a little expensive. Also, the absence of royalty fees should more than cover those third-party expenses. Mike was unsure of how much capital would be required to make the gym happen, but he was confident that he could raise the amount needed.

Given Ryan's interest, another option popped into Mike's mind - partner with Ryan on the venture, sharing the risks and rewards. Mike then thought about what some of the key uncertainties might be in starting a new gym with Ryan as a partner. Could Ryan deliver on his promise of bringing in a great training team? Could Mike find a facility in the area that would accommodate both short-term plans and long-term growth? Would they be able to generate enough membership to produce the revenues needed to offset the costs of running the operation and make a nice profit? What would Maddie think of the idea, particularly the part about partnering with Ryan? Mike had known Ryan for 10 years, he trusted him completely, the

Roses and the Jacksons had done a lot of social things together as couples, and Mike and Ryan were good friends, but they had never worked together. Good friends don't always make good business partners. Mike had a lot of thinking to do, so he and Ryan parted with Mike thanking Ryan for the new idea about starting his own gym.

Mike discussed the prospect with Maddie, and while she wasn't as enthused as Mike, she did see the potential and was willing to take the chance. She thought that partnering with Ryan was a good idea for sharing the risk. With Maddie on board, Mike went back to his value model, played a bit with two new choices – opening his own gym with Ryan as an employee, and opening his own gym with Ryan as a partner. With the new alternatives added, some of his value scales and swing weights needed to be adjusted, and Mike did more modeling of the key uncertainties. When he was done, he concluded that partnering with Ryan was his best choice.

Now it was time for Mike and Maddie to step back from the "best" analytical solution posed by the **FOCCUSSED** thinking approach and view the situation through another lens – a "socio" lens. Did the answer that their value model delivered match the feeling in their guts? The answer was *yes*. Did they think that they could be both friends and partners with the Jacksons without jeopardizing either relationship? The answer was *yes*. Now that this was becoming real, could Mike step away from his current job with assured income and jump into a new venture with both feet knowing that it might take a while to generate positive cash flow? The answer was a qualified *yes* since they had enough savings to get by for a while until the venture grew enough to pay the bills. Could they live with the high degree of uncertainty and stress that surrounded any new venture and still sleep nights? Again, the answer was *yes* (or at least a strong maybe!) With Maddie's concurrence, Mike then called Ryan to propose the partnership. Mike was pleased to learn that not only was Ryan willing to do it, Ryan was about to call Mike to suggest it himself! After some discussion of finances, they both concluded that, with some help from the bank, they could make this happen.

With that, a new business venture was born based on sound decision-making principles that were built upon Mike and Maddie's goals and objectives. Both were confident that they had made a good decision. And they both were confident that this would lead to a good outcome.

We've now worked our way through the technical part of the **FOCCUSSED** decision-making process, but there are still two topics that need to be addressed. First, we've learned analytical skills that enable us to build models with values and probabilities, but we haven't said much about how to obtain these inputs. Second, we've reached the point of producing a decision or a solution but, frequently, we still need to communicate the results to others. Data gathering and communication skills are among the set of capabilities that we refer to as "soft skills." The next chapters of this book will complete the **FOCCUSSED** process by addressing both *Data Gathering* and *Communications Skills*.

RAPID RECAP: SELECTING SOLUTIONS

- **Decisions are socio-technical processes** - We must consider not only the correct *analytical* solution (the technical side of the process), but equally important are the social and psychological aspects surrounding our decisions (the "socio" side of the process).

- **The FOCCUSSED decision-making process is iterative** - We should always try to generate better solutions than the apparent initial "best solution."

- **We need to know when to stop analyzing and when to start implementing solutions** – The key to this is requisite decision modeling and recognizing that "perfection is the enemy of good enough."

- **There are many barriers to successful implementation** - By first recognizing the barriers, we can develop innovative ways to overcome them.

"There is no greater joy than the burst of a solution to a problem."

~Daniel Keyes

Chapter 9: Eliciting Data: Making Your Decision-Making Processes More Productive

"Without data, you are just another person with an opinion."

"In God we trust. All others must bring data."

~W. Edwards Deming, *statistician, professor, author, lecturer, and consultant*

Since we rarely get to make and implement our decisions in a vacuum, we are often at the mercy of others for information needed to build our **FOCCUSSED** decision-making models or to present our results for their approval. In this chapter, we will talk about some of the soft skills that will be useful to us in Eliciting and gathering data for our models. The *Handbook for Decision Analysis* identifies several categories of soft skills that are useful to those analyzing decisions, and four of those relate to gathering information to properly frame and solve decision opportunities. We'll spend a little time discussing each. Those four skills are [25]:

- **Researching** – This includes gathering information to help us understand the problem's context, alternative modeling approaches, data sources, previous similar analyses, etc.

- **Interviewing** – This includes directly meeting with decision makers, subject matter experts, stakeholders, clients, and others who may set the objectives or who may have key information needed for the analysis.

- **Surveying** – At times, we can't get direct access to the parties with the information we need, particularly when they are in different locations. However, we might have the opportunity to survey them to get some of the critical opinions and facts.

- **Facilitating meetings** – Whether through small focus groups, one-time meetings, or recurring working sessions, this may be one of the best ways to gather information at any stage of the **FOCCUSSED** process. It may also be one of the most challenging.

STRUCTURED DATA GATHERING TECHNIQUES

Parnell [26] suggests a priority for the sources of information for our value and uncertainty models by defining four structured techniques for gathering information:

- **Platinum Standard** - The primary source of decision objectives are direct interviews with the decision maker and other senior leaders.

- **Gold Standard** – Approved documents such as strategic plans, mission and vision statements, operating policies, company directives, etc., serve as the foundation for the analysis.

- **Silver Standard** – When the supporting documents just aren't adequate, and when we can't get direct access to the decision makers and stakeholders themselves, we rely on group meetings with their representatives as our primary sources of information.

- **Combined Standard** – In most cases, we use a combination of the other three standards to bring together documents and information gathered through in-person techniques.

By applying our soft skills in conjunction with appropriate structuring techniques, we can be thoroughly prepared to execute the **FOCCUSSED** process. The first step is to better understand the four soft skills presented above.

Researching: Years ago, researching meant scouring the library for multiple references and relying on sources such as encyclopedias and journals for our information. The Internet has changed that model completely. We can "Google" virtually any topic and, in a matter of seconds, have pages of references related to the topic at hand. If you are trying to decide on which new car to buy, you can go to a database such as *Edmunds* for virtually every fact that you need to know about new cars. If you are feeling ill, sites such *WebMD* will offer more information than you can possibly comprehend to diagnose yourself (a very risky practice!). If you are a realtor trying to find a house for a client, the multiple listings can sort hundreds of houses in a specified area for those that meet your client's criteria. For Mike and Maddie looking at fitness franchises, there are thousands of possibilities that can be found by a search engine. For virtually any topic on which you do a search, *Wikipedia* can overwhelm you with information. But this wealth of information comes at a price. First of all, we have to determine the credibility of the source of the information. Anyone can post to *Wikipedia*, and the volumes of incorrect or biased information out there is scary. Second, we have to know when to stop collecting data and which sources of data will provide the best information. Third, even if we assume that all of the information is correct, as we apply it to the **FOCCUSSED** process, it still only provides us with what we've been calling **scoring** information. It doesn't help us with the **value** of the information since that is based on personal preference and cannot be looked up in a reference. Thus, while research is an important component of our decisions, it has many limitations and still requires us to determine what to use and what to ignore as we frame our problem, fine tune our objectives, develop alternatives, and evaluate our choices in terms of consequences, swaps, and solutions.

Interviewing: Interviews are most appropriate when we can get direct access to the senior decision makers and stakeholders who can provide direct guidance for our decision-making processes. Interviews are best limited to 30-60 minutes and should basically take the form of a conversation between the interviewer and the interviewee. A questionnaire should be developed in advance and tested on colleagues and friends to ensure that the questions are clearly understandable. During the interview, it is essential to keep careful notes, but that doesn't imply that you need a complete transcript of every word that is said. It is more important to hear what the participant says, re-state what you thought you heard to avoid misunderstandings, and document the most important ideas. It is helpful to probe for thorough responses to open-ended questions, and you should use any subject matter expertise that you have to ask challenging questions. You need to be prepared to respond to any questions that may be asked of you. Telling an occasional "war story" is okay to stimulate thought, but you have to be very careful to avoid dominating the discussion. Also, while it is sometimes hard to do, you must be careful not to impose your emotions and feelings on the participant. You need to be aware of your gestures and body language – participants pick up on them easily. At the same time, an interviewer must be sensitive to the participant's body language as it may give clues as to when to probe further. The interviewer also must be sensitive to the participant's emotions, not letting the participant think that his or her emotions are being ignored.

According to Thomas Kayser, in *Mining Group Gold* [27], you will encounter four different personality types as you conduct your interviews. Some participants will be very quiet, guarding their words and emotions; for these people, you will have to gently pull the information out of them. Some participants are very open with their words and emotions and they will want to tell you everything that they know; for these people, you will have to keep them on point and pay careful attention to the specific words behind their emotions. Some participants will be very direct in getting to the point, will speak quickly and confidently, and will have little patience for wasting time; for these people, it is critical to keep the interview moving and to avoid extended side conversations. Finally, some participants will be very sensitive to certain questions, will get upset very easily, and will show emotion openly. Their responses often avoid directly answering the questions, and their reasoning may be hard to follow; for these people, it is essential not to show frustration but, rather, to make them see that you understand their emotions.

Regardless of the nature of the interview, the most important key to success is preparation. Before the interview, practice on others to make sure that your questions are clear, establish tentative timelines for each question to help you stay on point, and know your exit criteria for the interview – that is, identify the most critical pieces of information that you need from the participant so that you can prioritize your questions. During the interview, go in with a plan, but be prepared to deviate from the plan in response to the participant. Be sensitive to the time constraints of the participant, particularly when interviewing a senior decision maker or manager. If possible, use a second person at the interview to take notes so that you can focus on the participant.

Surveying: We sometimes find ourselves in a situation where we need information from geographically dispersed experts, making interviews or group meetings impossible. In those circumstances, surveys can be an effective tool in gathering the required information. Surveys are best used with more junior people, and should range from 5-20 minutes - more than that and it is unlikely that you will get a response. In general, response rates to surveys are low; according to *SurveyGizmo*, internal surveys will generally receive a 30-40% response rate (or more) on average, compared to an average 10-15% response rate for external surveys. [28] There are many good online survey tools available such as *Survey Monkey, InsitefulSurveys, and SurveySystem*. When developing a survey, it is critical that the queries be unambiguous since the surveys will be completed without the benefit of being able to ask questions of the survey developer. As such, surveys are open to broad interpretation and even misinterpretation. The *Handbook of Decision Analysis* suggests the following steps in developing and implementing a survey [29]:

- Establish the goals and objectives of the survey.

- Determine who will be targeted for the survey.

- Determine the dissemination means (e.g., online web surveys, mail, e-mail, etc.).

- Prepare the survey questions and test them on others.

- Distribute the survey.

- Collect the data and analyze the results.

Based upon our experience, we consider the following to be best practices for surveys:

- Keep the questions simple with clear language and avoid compound questions with multiple parts. If necessary, provide definitions of any terms that may be interpreted differently by different participants.

- Establish response scales that are consistent and easy to use (e.g., don't have some scales go from low to high and others from high to low, etc.). There are many scale-types available such as **Likert Scales** that are well documented and tested.

- Keep the survey short to maintain interest; prioritize questions so that the most important are answered first, before participants tire of the effort.

- Test the survey before sending it out and revise questions that were ambiguous or confusing on the test run.

- Have a plan for following up on the survey and for analyzing the responses.

Used properly, surveys can be a useful adjunct to other data collection approaches or, if you have no other viable alternatives, can be used as the sole source of data. However, they can be expensive to conduct and the quality of the responses is often hard to assess.

Facilitating Meetings: There is no shortage of humorous quotes about meetings as shown below, and many of us try to avoid meetings like the plague:

"Meetings are indispensable when you don't want to do anything."

~John Kenneth Galbraith, *Economist*

"If you had to identify, in one word, the reason why the human race has not achieved, and never will achieve, its full potential, that word would be 'meetings.'"

~Dave Barry, *Humorist*

Fortunately, there is an opposing viewpoint. When done properly, meetings can be highly effective tools for advancing our decisions. Omar, in his best-selling book *The One Minute Meeting*, offers many great ideas for conducting effective meetings, and we will highlight some of those ideas in this chapter. In particular, we will focus here on concepts that are directly related to the steps in the **FOCCUSSED** decision-making process.

In his book, Omar describes three distinct categories of people who attend meetings [30]:

- Those who do not want to attend meetings since they perceive them as a waste of time;

- Those who love to attend meetings but for the wrong reasons such as seeing meetings as an easy way to get out of work;

- Those who see meetings not only as a necessary element of modern life, but, as a productive tool in reaching important goals that establish the intent for the meeting.

Hot Tip: *Meetings, if done correctly, can be exciting, productive, and empowering tools of modern corporate, industrial, and organizational practice. Yes, meetings can even be fun.*

Omar further describes many types of meetings to include scheduled meetings, opportunity/crisis meetings, planning meetings, problem-solving meetings, decision-making meetings, evaluation meetings, implementation meetings, and meetings that are combinations of the others. For our purposes, all of these are prevalent in one phase or another of **FOCCUSSED** decision making. Meetings can take on several formats to include guided discussions, free-for-alls, thinking on your feet sessions, and one-on-one meetings. In this chapter, we are going to discuss meetings such as small focus groups, but our primary emphasis will be on large facilitated group working sessions. There are some great references for facilitating meetings in the References section of this book, so we will just provide a quick overview without going into detail here and encourage those interested in honing their facilitation skills to read those books.

Focus Groups: Focus groups are most appropriate when dealing with a limited number of mid- to senior-level representatives of the decision makers and stakeholders. They typically last 2-4 hours and are very narrowly focused on a specific topic. They can include fully facilitated sessions, guided discussions, free-for-alls, or thinking on your feet sessions. They require careful note-taking and, frequently, they involve the use of automated groupware systems for simultaneously capturing ideas from all participants. If necessary, multiple "breakout sessions" can be used to address more than one topic, but the number of participants is usually too small to allow this while still having meaningful discussions. An experienced facilitator can help the group remain on topic and manage group behavior (we'll talk about this more later).

Facilitating larger working groups: There are times in our decision-making processes when we have to bring together larger groups of stakeholders and experts to gather the information we need and to make recommendations or reach decisions together. Sometimes, we can use a professional facilitator and, sometimes, we have to take on the role of facilitator ourselves. According to Roger Schwartz, in his book *The Skilled Facilitator*,

> "A facilitator is a person who helps a group free itself from internal obstacles or difficulties so that it may more efficiently and effectively pursue the achievement of desired outcomes."
> [31]

The facilitator can play different roles to include a coach, a consultant, a trainer, an evaluator, a mediator, or a leader/manager, and sometimes the facilitator must play multiple roles. That is particularly challenging since it is very difficult to orchestrate a meeting in an unbiased, neutral manner while offering expert content opinions as well. We will focus on exploring the role of the facilitator as the manager of the group process and not address the role as a content matter expert.

CHARACTERISTICS OF A GOOD FACILITATOR

According to Kayser [32], the facilitator manages the group processes and intervenes when necessary to keep the group on target. The facilitator helps the group to frame the questions, but he/she has to be careful because the manner in which the facilitator frames and probes open-ended questions can greatly affect the answers. Part of the facilitator's job is to obtain the facts and to ascertain the level of confidence that the participant has in his/her ability to answer. That includes distinguishing among facts, feelings, and emotions, as well as finding out what is known, what is assumed, and what are merely opinions or conjecture. Contrast this with the role of a subject matter expert who is there to provide content and expertise on the topics under discussion. Kayser describes the following facilitator tasks:

- Assist in the group process and set a positive tone for the meetings

- Focus the group efforts and energies

- Gain group commitment and encourage participation when appropriate

- Define needs, issues, and concerns

- Manage expectations and conflicts

- Keep the group on topic and on schedule

- Analyze and make suggestions when appropriate

- Keep notes (either yourself or, preferably, a note-taker) and summarize and synthesize discussions.

The facilitator must ask questions carefully and consistently while using clear vocabulary, must ask for feedback, and must clarify and elaborate as needed. The facilitator must listen to the responses carefully while using listening techniques such as paraphrasing, repeating word for word, etc. At the same time, the facilitator must be cognizant of his/her body language and expressions so as not to raise concerns among the participants. As a facilitator, it is your job to:

- Stimulate the conversation

- Understand but not evaluate participants' feelings

- Refocus the group based upon desired outcomes

- Stay neutral on content

- Stay focused on the situation, not on any one individual's or the group's behaviors

- Balance group participation.

Once again, quoting that great American philosopher, Yogi Berra,

"If you don't know where you are going, you'll wind up someplace else and not know how you got there."

It is the job of the facilitator to make sure that the group knows where it is going and to take the right steps to lead it there.

In our many years of facilitating group decisions, we've discovered that not all groups are as easy to work with as others. In fact, we've often come across what can best be described as dysfunctional behaviors within groups. These include:

- Silence and non-participation

- Dominating personalities

- Conflict

- Chronic objectors to the process

- Late arrivals

- Side conversations

- Rambling answers

- Inappropriate comments.

Several of the above make it clear that many meetings may not always go as smoothly as we would like but, in reality, disagreement within a group is a positive thing. If we channel it into an open exchange of information with the goal of informed consensus, we can use such disagreement to our advantage.

Hot Tip: *Clashes within your group are healthy provided they are open, do not pull the group from the agenda, do not fall into name calling or personality baiting, and provided the leader remains in control.*

We won't go into detail on how to handle each of these behaviors, and most are discussed in Omar's *The One Minute Meeting*, but we do believe that some general principles apply:

- Be friendly, but firm in confronting the behavior

- Focus on the behavior, not the individual

- Highlight the impact of disruptive behaviors

- Suggest more functional behaviors

- Avoid sustained one-on-one arguments or exchanges

- Use others in the group to help

- Never display your anger to the group, even if justified

- Maintain your sense of humor and use it with the group

- Stay aware of time and schedules

- Relax and have fun; enjoy your work!

OMAR'S TIPS FOR BETTER MEETINGS

Whether you are the facilitator or just the organizer of the meeting, there are some important steps to follow. First, **develop a meeting plan**. Poorly planned meetings waste time, energy, and other resources, and can negatively impact morale. Second, **create an agenda** or you will have chaos. An agenda is simply a statement as to the intent of the meeting, how it will be handled, and the goal to be achieved. It should include a timeline for each phase of the meeting. It can also be used to prioritize the outcomes of the meeting. Design the agenda in a way that, if you run out of time, which will happen on occasion, you'll at least be able to cover the primary topics. These are your exit criteria for the meeting. Third, **select the attendees**. It is best to have a group with varying perspectives that will lead to informative, sometimes contentious discussions but, will get all of the information needed out on the table. It is a best practice to learn as much as you can about the backgrounds and personalities of the attendees in advance - who will be the real experts, who will be the dominant personalities, who will cause you the most difficulty, etc. If the same people are expected to attend a series of meetings, it is essential to have their commitment to attend all meetings and not send substitutes. It can be extremely disruptive to the purpose of the group if new participants constantly have to be re-educated on what happened previously. Fourth, if possible, **check out the meeting facilities** and decide upon the room layout that will be most effective. Whenever possible, we prefer circular tables which eliminate the "head of the table" position, thus diminishing the role that "rank" will play. Determine if you have Internet connectivity, sufficient white boards or easels and markers for note taking, sufficient electrical outlets and extension cords, laptop connectivity to projectors (if needed), and so forth. If the meeting will be long, make sure arrangements are made for snacks, beverages, or meals, or that there is adequate time in the agenda to take a break for meals. Fifth, **prepare the presentation material for the meeting carefully**. In the next chapter, we will discuss principles of good communication – use them! Have professional looking slides and check for spelling errors. It is surprising how distracted a group can become by small, but noticeable errors. Present materials in a way that is most comfortable for the participants, not necessarily most comfortable for you. Sixth, and most important, **be prepared.** Know your material, practice the phases of the session, and have realistic expectations that you can manage. It is a best practice to look at everything that you are going to present and ask yourself, how can any of this be misinterpreted? A version of Murphy's Law will inevitably apply – if something can be misconstrued, it will be misconstrued. Anticipate questions, even off-the-wall questions, and be prepared to address them. If you are well prepared, you can be confident knowing that you will be able to answer almost any question that arises. It is okay to say "I don't know" and assure participants that you will get the answers that you don't have – but make sure that you follow through quickly. If you are well prepared, you can have a positive attitude towards the group. Nothing disrupts a group more than a "baditude" of the facilitator, and participants will quickly pick up on your body language, your expressions, and the inflections in your voice. Negative thoughts can be a "buzz kill," so you must develop enthusiasm and let that energy, excitement, and passion for your subject show through. You will be amazed by how infectious a positive or negative attitude can become, so it is critical that you keep things positive.

We've now covered various means that you can use to get the facts, opinions, values, uncertainties, and other information that might be useful to us in our **FOCCUSSED** decision-making ventures. We have one last **FOCCUSSED** topic to cover – disseminating and communicating our results.

RAPID RECAP: ELICITING DATA – MAKING YOUR DECISION-MAKING PROCESSES MORE MEANINGFUL AND PRODUCTIVE

- We are often at the mercy of others for information needed to build our **FOCCUSSED** decision-making models or to present our results for their approval.

- In addition to strong analytical skills, it is helpful to be competent in **soft skills** to include **researching, interviewing, surveying, and facilitating** meetings.

- When making decisions, we may find ourselves in the role of a **facilitator of group working sessions or meetings,** and we must be prepared for that role. The facilitator can play different roles to include a coach, a consultant, a trainer, an evaluator, a mediator, or a leader/manager, and sometimes the facilitator must play multiple roles.

- Whether you are the facilitator or the organizer of a meeting, there are some important steps to follow. These include: **develop a meeting plan, create an agenda, select the attendees, check out the meeting facilities, prepare the presentation material for the meeting carefully,** and **prepare for questions.**

"You will never see eye-to-eye if you never meet face-to-face."

~Warren Buffett, *Chairman and CEO, Berkshire Hathaway*

NOTES:

CHAPTER 10: DISSEMINATING AND COMMUNICATING YOUR DECISIONS

*"I know that you believe you understand what you think I said, but,
I am not sure you realize that what you heard is not what I meant."*

-Attributed to Robert McCloskey, U.S. State Department spokesman,
by Marvin Kalb, CBS reporter, in *TV Guide*, 31 March 1984,
citing an unspecified press briefing during the Vietnam War.

This chapter is all about communicating, so why did we title it using the word **D**isseminating? We are not ashamed to admit that we needed a word that started with a "D" to make the FOCCUSSED acronym fit, and there weren't very many good synonyms for communicating that started with a "D!" "Disseminating" comes closest but, in reality, our focus will be on communicating. A rose by any other name …

Some of you might be thinking to yourselves, why is there even a chapter on communications in a book about decision making? As ridiculously unclear as the opening quote is, in our experience, communications such as that are not isolated events. As we help others make decisions, we come across communications that are confused, garbled, and just plain nonsensical far too often. For some of you, your decisions will go no further than yourselves but, for many of you, you'll need to communicate your decisions to your spouses, your partners, your clients, your investors, your bankers, etc.

What Determines Good Communication?

Good communications are about the receiver, the message, and the sender. If the receiver does not understand the message, there has been no communication. Sometimes, we just talk past each other while thinking that the message is getting through. But, in our experience, we find that how we communicate the results of decision-making processes is often the most critical part of the analysis process and, unfortunately, it is the most commonly deficient part of the process. If we want to do it right, we need to start thinking about how we will communicate our decisions *before* our detailed analysis is conducted. We believe in a corollary of the Covey philosophy mentioned earlier, "in the beginning, think of the end." It goes without saying that it helps greatly to perform credible, defensible analysis using the best methods, techniques, tools, and technologies available but, in our opinion, when the analysis is finished you are no more than 50% done.

Credible, quality analysis is very important but it is not all that is needed for success. To best communicate with decision makers, we recommend that you focus on the story behind the analysis, and then tell the story in a way that is understandable to the decision makers and other stakeholders who may be involved. This takes time and careful planning. Sometimes, we become so enamored with the effort and sophistication that we put into our analyses that we want everyone else to know how smart we are and we show them every gory detail of our decision-making process. This is rarely the best thing to do.

What we find in the consulting world is that each decision maker has a different learning style and preference for information. Those going through the kinds of processes described in this book tend to present their results to others in ways that are most comfortable to themselves. What we should be doing instead is to tailor our message to the decision makers and stakeholders. For simplicity, we will use the term decision maker to refer to the receiver even though it may be any of the types of people mentioned above. Some best practices for doing this include:

- "Seek first to understand then to be understood." [33] We need to ask unambiguous questions and document the answers carefully. We need to listen to the questions asked of us and answer those questions briefly and clearly.

- Our communications should be **tailored** to a specific purpose and decision maker.

- The process of determining the information to convey should be comfortable and **efficient** for the decision maker.

- The communication process should make information **accessible** so that the decision maker can "drill down" into the details of the analysis (if desired.)

- The decision maker should understand what **degree of confidence** to place in the findings, which means that we need to identify our assumptions and uncertainties.

- The decision maker should understand the **implications for action.**

DEVELOPING COMMUNICATIONS STRATEGIES

There are several factors that we should consider when developing our communications strategy:

- *Cognitive style of the decision maker:* Some people love seeing the numbers, while others are more visually oriented and prefer charts and diagrams. Some want to be led by the hand through the steps of the analysis, while others want to hear what we call "the bottom line up front," or the BLUF. How do we determine which style is best in each case? Ask! Ask those who have worked with the decision maker before or even directly ask the decision maker.

- *The decision context:* We should consider the context of the decision and the decision briefing itself. Is it a stand-alone presentation, or is it a piece of something much larger? Are we seeking guidance, or are we presenting results? Is the decision time-sensitive, or do we have the luxury of making several passes in figuring out the best solution?

- *The nature of what is to be communicated:* Are we only trying to convey information? Are we presenting a decision that, for all intents and purposes, has already been made? Or, are we asking that a specific decision be made?

When giving a formal presentation, most of us have a tendency to use too many presentation slides with too much information on each slide. It is far better to use fewer and better slides that focus on the most important messages that we are trying to send. As a rule of thumb, if you use more than 10-15 slides for a 30 minute presentation, you probably have too much information. It is helpful to put a summary of the key message on every chart and, above all, present the message, not the methodology.

Edward Tufte is *the* expert on visual display of quantitative information. Tufte describes graphical excellence as a well-designed presentation of interesting data that is a matter of substance, of statistics, and of design. Graphical excellence consists of complex ideas communicated with clarity, precision, and efficiency. It gives to the viewer the greatest number of ideas in the shortest time with the least ink in the smallest space. [34] Tufte provides very useful guidelines. His advice to include words, numbers, and drawings is especially important if there are many decision makers and stakeholders, since each may have preferred learning styles. Tufte's suggestions include:

- Have a properly chosen format and design.

- Use words, numbers, and drawings together.

- Reflect a balance, proportion, and sense of relevant scale.

- Display an accessible complexity of detail.

- Have a history to tell.

- Draw in a professional manner with careful reproduction.

- Avoid "chart junk" (unnecessary lines, designs, cross-hatching, etc.).

While Tufte's advice is general, we have some of our own specific advice for the types of decision-making processes presented in this book. There are unique challenges in communicating the results of a **FOCCUSSED** study:

- Value trade-offs are difficult for some decision makers. Decision makers tend to think in terms of absolute value, while most decisions involve relative value assessments. It is often hard to get decision makers to understand how you compared "apples and oranges."

- Communicating relative weights is uncomfortable for some people. It is helpful to use examples from everyday life. Use the term "swing weights" to distinguish the weights you use from importance weights.

- Communicating probabilistic information is particularly challenging. We need to keep things simple and focus on getting the "conditional" nature of probabilities correct.

- Show the results of "what if" analysis. Focus on the changes in the data that change the decision.

- Show the results from the perspective of different stakeholders (if appropriate).

- Be prepared to adjust what you have prepared. You have to be able to think on your feet and be willing to modify your presentation in order to accommodate changing circumstances.

Hot Tip: *Computers are great tools in helping us do the math behind the decisions. However, asserting that "The computer says this is the best decision" is **never** a valid defense of a decision.*

We always have to keep certain things in mind when our role is that of a facilitator or an analyst, but not the decision maker: it is our job to communicate meaningful recommendations to the decision maker, the decision maker is free to take or ignore those recommendations, and we cannot take it personally when he/she chooses the latter.

Hot Tip: *When making recommendations for decisions, never forget what has come to be known as **the golden rule of management** – the one with the gold makes the rules. The decision maker can choose to totally ignore your recommendations, and that is okay.*

In conclusion, we've spent the vast majority of this book learning how to be a **FOCCUSSED** decision maker. But, it is equally important to be a good communicator. Over the years, we've seen far too many great analyses be rejected because of the inability to communicate some really great ideas to others. Whether you are a sole proprietor making your own decisions, a professional services provider helping your clients to make better decisions, a budding entrepreneur with many varied interests, or any other person with difficult decisions to make, the ability to communicate your ideas to others is an invaluable asset to have in your toolkit.

RAPID RECAP: COMMUNICATING YOUR DECISIONS TO OTHERS

- When it comes to communicating results of decisions, as suggested by Covey earlier, **in the beginning, think of the end.**

- Communicating results of a **FOCCUSSED** decision-making process:

  o Is one of the most critical parts of the process

  o Is the most commonly deficient part of the process

  o Should start before analysis is conducted.

- Use principles of graphical excellence to prepare your presentations.

"The single biggest problem in communication is the illusion that it has taken place."

~George Bernard Shaw

NOTES:

Chapter 11: Foccussed Decision Making Wrap-Up

Congratulations! You are now prepared to apply **FOCCUSSED** decision making to your personal life and your business life. You've learned how to:

- **I**dentify and properly frame the decision or problem at hand.

- Specify the **o**bjectives, goals, and values that you are trying to achieve.

- Develop creative, meaningful **c**hoices from which to select.

- Evaluate the **c**onsequences of selecting each alternative using your goals, objectives, and values.

- Think about the key **u**ncertainties that could impact the decision.

- Understand the **s**waps that you are willing to make.

- Develop an approach for implementing your **s**olution.

- **E**licit the data you'll need from a variety of sources.

- **D**isseminate and communicate your decisions to others.

By applying the principles of Value-Focused Thinking, you are well-equipped to make good decisions that are consistent with your preferences, alternatives, and information.

You know how to use decision hierarchies, stakeholders' issue identification matrices, and vision statements to frame the problem properly.

You know how to distinguish between your fundamental objectives and your means objectives, and how to turn them into value hierarchies, value measures, and value scales that can later be used to identify and evaluate the consequences of your choices.

You know how to develop a creative set of choices and alternatives using divergent and convergent thinking, and how to flesh them out in strategy tables.

You know how to think about uncertainty as a state of information, and about how to explore uncertainties using simple decision trees and expected value calculations.

You know how to prioritize your goals, objectives, and value measures using swing weights, and how to use those weights in combination with your value measures to articulate the swaps and trade-offs that you are willing to make.

You know how to bring all of the above pieces together to produce solutions and take on opportunities that are consistent with the elements of a good decision.

You know the basics of different approaches to gathering the data you will need to perform your analyses such as researching, interviewing, surveying, and facilitating groups.

And, finally, you know the basics of disseminating and communicating your decisions to others when needed.

Now, all that is left for you to do is to go out there and practice what we've preached. Apply the techniques to your personal decisions, to your investment decisions, to your own business decisions, and to your clients' decisions. You can do it, and you can do it well. Applying what you've learned is not difficult, is low risk, and can be extremely rewarding in many ways.

Welcome to our world of the **FOCCUSSED** decision maker.

TERRY and OMAR

NOTES:

Appendix A: Solutions For Math Nerds To The Chapter 6 Probability Problems

1. You are in a room that has 50 people in it (counting yourself). What is the probability that there are two people in the room that have the same birthday (day and month, not year)?

Solution: If there is one person in the room, the chances are 364 out of 365 that the next person will not match birthdays. When a third person enters, there are 363 out of 365 days that don't match since there are two other people. To calculate the probability that the second person doesn't match and the third person doesn't match, we must multiply the probabilities together to get the probability of no match since this is a joint event. To get the probability of a match, we must subtract the probability of no match from 1.0 (or 100%) since the events are mutually exclusive and collectively exhaustive. The math continues in the same manner as each additional person compares birthdays as can be seen in the spreadsheet below. Note that once there are 22 people in the room, the probability exceeds 50%!

Birthday Problem - Probability that 2 people have same date and month for birthdays

Number of People in the Room																			
Number of people in the room	1	2	3	4	5	6	7	8	9	10	11	12	13	14	15	16	17	18	19	20
Number of Days that don't match	364	363	362	361	360	359	358	357	356	355	354	353	352	351	350	349	348	347	346	345
Total days in the year	365	365	365	365	365	365	365	365	365	365	365	365	365	365	365	365	365	365	365	365
Probability of no match for next person	1.00	0.99	0.99	0.99	0.99	0.98	0.98	0.98	0.97	0.97	0.97	0.96	0.96	0.96	0.96	0.95	0.95	0.95	0.95	
Cumulative probability of no match for next person		0.99	0.98	0.97	0.96	0.94	0.93	0.91	0.88	0.86	0.83	0.81	0.78	0.75	0.72	0.68	0.65	0.62	0.59	0.56
Cumulative probability of a match = (1- probability of no match)		0.01	0.02	0.03	0.04	0.06	0.07	0.09	0.12	0.14	0.17	0.19	0.22	0.25	0.28	0.32	0.35	0.38	0.41	0.44

Number of People in the Room																			
Number of people in the room	21	22	23	24	25	26	27	28	29	30	31	32	33	34	35	36	37	38	39	40
Number of Days that don't match	344	343	342	341	340	339	338	337	336	335	334	333	332	331	330	329	328	327	326	325
Total days in the year	365	365	365	365	365	365	365	365	365	365	365	365	365	365	365	365	365	365	365	365
Probability of no match for next person	0.94	0.94	0.93	0.93	0.93	0.93	0.92	0.92	0.92	0.92	0.91	0.91	0.91	0.90	0.90	0.90	0.90	0.89	0.89	
Cumulative probability of no match for next person	0.52	0.49	0.46	0.43	0.40	0.37	0.35	0.32	0.29	0.27	0.25	0.23	0.20	0.19	0.17	0.15	0.14	0.12	0.11	0.10
Cumulative probability of a match = (1- probability of no match)	0.48	0.51	0.54	0.57	0.60	0.63	0.65	0.68	0.71	0.73	0.75	0.77	0.80	0.81	0.83	0.85	0.86	0.88	0.89	0.90

Probability exceeds 50% ⟹

2. In front of you are three chests, each with an upper and lower drawer. One chest has a gold coin in each drawer, one has a silver coin in each drawer, and one has one gold and one silver coin in the drawers (but you don't know if the gold is in the upper or lower drawer). You select a chest

at random, pick one drawer, and see a gold coin. What is the probability that if you open the second drawer in the same chest, you will see another gold coin?

Solution: We can solve this using Bayes' Rule (see Chapter 6). We are looking for the probability of seeing a gold coin in drawer 2 of a chest in which we've seen a gold coin in drawer 1 of that chest. We will use the following notation:

P(GG)= Probability of picking the chest with two gold coins = 1/3

P(SS) = Probability of picking the chest with two silver coins = 1/3

P(SG) = Probability of picking the chest with one silver and one gold coin = 1/3

Let:

$P(G1|SS)$= Probability of a gold coin in the 1st drawer given we're in the SS chest = 0

$P(G_1|GG)$= Probability of a gold coin in the 1st drawer given we're in the GG chest = 1.0

$P(G_1|GS)$= Probability of getting a gold coin in the 1st drawer given we're in the GS chest = .50

$P(GG|G1)$= Probability of a gold coin in the 2nd drawer given that there was a gold coin in the 1st drawer. This is what we are looking for. According to Bayes' Rule:

$$P(GG|G_1) = \frac{P(G_1|GG) \times P(GG)}{P(G_1)}$$

We know the two terms in the numerator, but the term in the denominator is the tricky term. We can calculate $P(G_1)$= Probability of getting a gold coin in the 1st drawer by calculating all of the ways that we can get a gold coin in the 1st drawer and adding them up. That calculation would be:

$$P(G_1) = P(G1|GG) \times P(GG) + P(G1|GS) \times P(GS) + P(G1|SS) \times P(SS)$$
$$= 1.0 \times 1/3 + 1/2 \times 1/3 + 0 \times 1/3 = 1/3 + 1/6 = \frac{1}{2}$$

Therefore, from the Bayes Rule equation, $P(GG|G_1) = (1.0 \times 1/3)/(1/2) = 2/3$

There is a 2/3 chance that the second coin will be gold!

3. You are visiting Las Vegas and are playing the roulette wheel. A red number has come up seven times in a row. If you were betting on the next spin, would you bet on red or black?

Solution: No special math needed here. If we assume each trial is independent, it doesn't matter whether we bet on red or black since:

$$P(black) = P(red) = .50 \text{ (ignoring the 00 on the wheel for simplicity)}$$

If we assume that the wheel is biased and that is why we saw seven red numbers in a row, we should bet on red. There is no logic that favors betting on black. It makes no sense to reason that "a black is due" if the events are truly independent.

4. You are a winning contestant on "Let's Make a Deal." You are playing for a new car. There are five keys on a rack; if you select the key that starts the car, you win it. You've decided to pick key #1. The game show host tells you that he is going to make things easier for you to win, and he tells you that the winning key is not key #2 (he always tells the truth, and he knows which one is the winning key). He then offers you the

opportunity to swap the key you selected, key #1, for one of the remaining keys, #3, #4, or #5. Do you make the swap?

Solution: Conceptually, this problem is the same as the three chests with coins problem, and the solution is again found via Bayes Rule. Let the probability that a key starts the car (in this case, key #1) be represented as $P(1)$. Initially,

$$P(1) = P(2) = P(3) = P(4) = P(5) = 1/5$$

We will use quotation marks to indicate what the host says. For example, if the host says that it is not key #2 that starts the car, we use $P(\text{"not 2"})$ to denote that. The probability that the host says that it is not key #2 when the actual winning key is key #1 would be denoted as $P(\text{"not 2"}|1)$. Let's then compare the probabilities of winning if you keep key #1 to the probability of winning if you swap for key #3. The probability that key #1 is the correct key given that the host says it is not key #2 would be calculated using Bayes Rule as:

$$P(1|\text{"not2"}) = \frac{P(\text{"not 2"}|1) \times P(1)}{P(\text{"not 2"})}$$

For the first term in the numerator, if the actual winning key is key #1, there is a 1/4 chance that he says it is not key #2 since he has four keys to choose from – keys #2, #3, #4, or #5. For the second term in the numerator, this is just the prior probability of key #1 starting the car, or 1/5. The term in the denominator is calculated from all of the ways that the host can say that it is not key #2, or;

$$P(\text{"not 2"}) = P(\text{"not 2"}|1) \times P(1) + P(\text{"not 2"}|2) \times P(2) + P(\text{"not 2"}|3) \times P(3)$$
$$+ P(\text{"not 2"}|4) \times P(4) + + P(\text{"not 2"}|5) \times P(5)$$
$$= 1/4 \times 1/5 + 0 \times 1/5 + 1/3 \times 1/5 + 1/3 \times 1/5 + 1/3 \times 1/5 = 1/4$$

Therefore, from Bayes Rule,

$$P(1|\text{"not 2"}) = \frac{1/4 \times 1/5}{1/4} = 1/5$$

Now compare this with the probability for the potential swap key, key #3:

$$P(3|\text{"not2"}) = \frac{P(\text{"not 2"}|3) \times P(3)}{P(\text{"not 2"})} = \frac{1/3 \times 1/5}{1/4} = 4/15$$

Since swapping for key #3 has a higher probability than keeping key #1, you should make the swap. And if the host offers a second similar swap, take it again. The chances of winning go up each time. Of course, you have to be willing to live with the regret of having given away the winning key if you swap and the key you gave away starts the car. Remember, we can make a good decision and still have a bad outcome!

Appendix B: Omar's Deal Flip Template

Deal Flip Formula:

Asking Price (AP): $	
After Repair Value (ARV): $	
www.relar.com Value: $	
www.valuationvision.com Value: $	
Appraised value: $	
Review appraised value: $	
Your Maximum Allowable Offer: * $	
(MAO)	
Offer 1: $	
Counter 1: $	
Counter 2: $	
Counter 3: $	
Accepted Offer: $	
-Holding Costs (HC): $	
(HC) should be estimated at 10% of asking price	
-Cost of Acquisition Funds: $	
-Rehab Costs: $	
-Rehab Timeline in actual days :	
Estimated Selling Price: $	
Estimated selling timeline in days:	
+Actual Selling Price: $	
Actual days it took to sell:	
-Selling Closing Costs: $	
Minimum Spread: $ 25,000.00	
+Actual Total Spread: $	

APPENDIX C: OUR FAVORITE COMMERCIAL OFF-THE-SHELF DECISION ANALYSIS SOFTWARE PACKAGES

Crystal Ball - This is an Excel add-in produced by *Oracle* that allows for both deterministic and probabilistic analysis using Monte Carlo simulation.

DPL - This stands for **Decision Programming Language** and is produced by *Syncopation*. The software is an excellent tool for the uncertainty phases of the **FOCCUSSED** process, and it can be used to develop strategy tables, decision trees and more sophisticated influence diagrams.

HIVIEW - This is a great package from *Catalyze, Ltd.* for the deterministic (non-probabilistic) phase of **FOCCUSSED** decision making. You can build value hierarchies, value scales, perform swing weighting, etc. It offers some great displays for communicating results.

Logical Decisions – This is an easy to use package from *Logical Decisions, Inc.*, that that can be used to develop value hierarchies, value curves, and swing weights, and to perform a limited degree of probabilistic analysis.

Microsoft Excel - Excel allows you to create and tailor your own models for performing **FOCCUSSED** decision making at a relatively low cost. With the Solver add-on, you can also evaluate optimization decisions.

Precision Tree - This is an Excel add-in produced by *Palisade Corporation* that provides capability for probabilistic analysis using decision trees and influence diagrams.

@Risk - This is an Excel add-in produced by *Palisade Corporation* that enables probabilistic analysis using Monte Carlo simulation.

ENDNOTES

[1] Napoleon I, *The Officer's Manual, Napoleon's Maxims of War*, annotated by D'Aguilar, G. C. (George Charles), 1862.

[2] Scott Adams, *Dogbert's Top Secret Management Handbook*, (New York: Harper Business, 1996).

[3] Ralph Keeney, "Making Better Decision Makers," *Decision Analysis*, Vol. 1, No. 4, pp. 193-204, Dec 2004.

[4] John Hammond, Ralph Keeney, and Howard Raiffa, *Smart Choices*, (Boston: Harvard University Press, 1999), pp. 17-18.

[5] James Adams, *Conceptual Blockbusting: A Guide to Better Ideas,* (Stanford: The Portable Stanford, 1979), p. 23.

[6] Charles Kepner and Benjamin Tregoe, *The New Rational Manager*, (Princeton: Princeton Research Press, 1981), p. 38.

[7] Gregory Parnell, Terry Bresnick, Steven Tani, and Eric Johnson, *Handbook of Decision Analysis* (Hoboken, NJ: John Wiley & Sons, 2013), p. 118.

[8] Ralph Keeney, *Value-Focused Thinking* (Cambridge, MA: Harvard University Press, 1992), pp. 3-6.

[9] Vilfredo Pareto, Alfred Page, *Translation of Manuale di Economia Politica ("Manual of Political Economy")*, (1971).

[10] Gary Klein, "Sources of Power: How People Make Decisions," (Cambridge, MA: MIT Press, 1989) pp. 1-30,

[11] Herbert A. Simon, Administrative Behavior: *a Study of Decision-Making Processes in Administrative Organization, (New York: Macmillan, 1947)*.

[12] *Handbook of Decision Analysis*, p. 150-152.

[13] James Adams, pp. 10-11.

[14] *Intelligence Community Directive 203, Analytic Standards*, pp.2-4 (http://www.DNI.Gov)

[15] Keeney, p.141.

[16] "What Are the Odds of a Shark Attack?" *International Wildlife Museum Website*, (http://www.thewildlifemuseum.org/exhibits/sharks/odds-of-a-shark-attack/)

[17] Benjamin Franklin, "Letter from Benjamin Franklin to Joseph Priestly," (London, 19 September 1772).

[18] Lawrence D. Phillips, "Decision Conferencing" In *Advances in Decision Analysis: From Foundations to Applications, Ward Edwards, Ralph Miles, and Detlof von Winterfeldt, (eds.)* (Cambridge, UK: Cambridge University Press, 2007).

[19] Steven Covey, *The 7 Habits of Highly Effective People,* (New York: Simon and Schuster, 2004).

[20] *Handbook of Decision Analysis*, p. 342.

[21] Omar Periu, *The One Minute Meeting*, (Boca Raton, FL: Omar Periu International, Inc., 2004), p38.

[22] Lawrence D. Phillips, *Acta Psychologica*, 1984, Vol. 56, pp. 29-48.

[23] M.P. Singh (2005), *Quote Unquote (A Handbook of Quotations)*, p. 223 from Wikipedia (https://en.wikipedia.org/wiki/Perfect_is_the_enemy_of_good).

[24] Encyclopedia Britannica (http://www.britannica.com/topic/Occams-razor/Occam's Razor).

[25] *Handbook of Decision Analysis*, pp. 4-8.

[26] *Handbook of Decision Analysis*, pp. 139-140.

[27] Thomas A. Kayser, *Mining Group Gold,* (New York: McGraw Hill, 1990) pp.190-192.

[28] *SurveyGizmo*, July 27, 2015, (https://www.surveygizmo.com/survey-blog/survey-response-rates/).

[29] *Handbook of Decision Analysis*, pp. 78-80.

[30] Omar Periu, p51.

[31] Roger Schwartz, *The Skilled Facilitator*, (San Francisco: Jossey Bass, 2002), p51.

[32] Kayser, pp. 29-36.

[33] Covey, Habit #5.

[34] Edward R. Tufte, The Visual Display of Quantitative Information, (Cheshire, CT: Graphics Press, 1983), p51.

References

Decision Analysis and Decision Making

Clemen, R. *Making Hard Decisions*, 2nd Edition. Belmont, CA: Wadsworth Publishing Company Press, 1996.

Celona, J. and McNamee, P. *Decision Analysis for the Professional, 4th Edition*. Stanford, CA: SmartOrg, Inc., 2005.

Edwards, W, Miles, R., and Winterfeldt, D., Editors. *Advances in Decision Analysis*. New York: Cambridge University Press, 2007.

Hammond, J., Keeney, R. and Raiffa, H. *Smart Choices*. Boston: Harvard University Press, 1999.

Howard, R. A. and Matheson, J.E., Editors. *The Principles & Applications of Decision Analysis*, Volumes I & II. Stanford, CA: Strategic Decisions Group, 1983.

Keeney, R.L. *Value-Focused Thinking: A Path to Creative Decisionmaking*. Cambridge, Massachusetts: Harvard University Press, 1992.

Keeney, R.L. and Raiffa H. *Decisions with Multiple Objectives: Preferences and Value Trade-offs*. New York: Wiley & Sons, Inc., 1976.

Kirkwood, C. W. *Strategic Decision Making: Multiobjective Decision Analysis with Spreadsheets*. Belmont, California: Duxbury Press, 1997.

Matheson, D. and Matheson, J.E. *The Smart Organization: Creating Value Through Strategic R&D*, Harvard Business School Press, 1998.

Parnell, G., Bresnick, T., Tani, S., and Johnson E. *Handbook of Decision Analysis*. Hoboken, NJ: Wiley & Sons, 2014.

Parnell, G. S., Driscoll, P. J., and Henderson D. L., Editors. *Decision Making for Systems Engineering and Management*, 2nd Edition, Andrew P. Sage, Editor. Hoboken, NJ: Wiley & Sons, Inc., 2011.

Other Great References

Adams, J. Conceptual Blockbusting: A Guide to Better Ideas. Stanford, CA: The Portable Stanford, 1979.

Covey, S. The 7 Habits of Highly Effective People. New York: Simon and Schuster, 2004.

Kayser, T. Mining Group Gold. New York: McGraw Hill, 1990.

Kepner, C. and Tregoe, B. The New Rational Manager. Princeton NJ: Princeton Research Press, 1981)

Periu, O. Get R.E.A.L. & Get Rich. Boca Raton, FL: Omar Periu International, Inc., 2004.

Periu, O. The One-Minute Meeting. Boca Raton, FL: Omar Periu International, Inc., 2007.

Schwartz, R. The Skilled Facilitator. San Francisco: Jossey Bass, 2002.

Tufte, E. The Visual Display of Quantitative Information. Cheshire, CT: Graphics Press, 1983.

INDEX

Made in the USA
Lexington, KY
12 April 2016